THE ULTIMATE GUIDE

Titan
MAGAZINES

Solo: A Star Wars Story
The Ultimate Guide
ISBN: 9781785869587

Editor Jonathan Wilkins
Senior Editor Martin Eden
Art Director Oz Browne
Publishing Manager Darryl Tothill
Publishing Director Chris Teather
Operations Director Leigh Baulch
Executive Director Vivian Cheung
Publisher Nick Landau

Published by Titan
A division of
Titan Publishing Group Ltd.,
144 Southwark Street,
London, SE1 0UP

First Edition November 2018
10 9 8 7 6 5 4 3 2 1

Printed in China.

Acknowledgments
Titan would like to thank Brett Rector and Michael Siglain at
Lucasfilm for all of their invaluable help in putting this volume
together.

CONTENTS

RON HOWARD

DIRECTOR ON SET

The acclaimed director on calling the shots on *Solo: A Star Wars Story*.

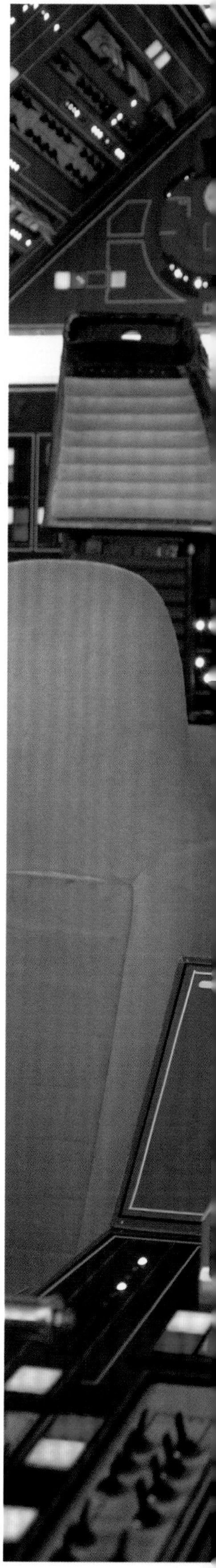

With a career spanning more than six decades in film and TV, movie-making runs in legendary Hollywood director Ron Howard's veins. Here, he reveals how his long association with the *Star Wars* universe and creator George Lucas dates back much further than his first day on the *Solo: A Star Wars Story* set, to his early days on the cult classic *American Graffiti* (1973) and the 1988 blockbuster, *Willow*.

You had a foretelling conversation with George Lucas some years ago. Can you tell us about that?

George was shooting *American Graffiti* in 1972, the summer after my senior year in high school, and I had a part in it. I was amazed by the whole thing. I had grown up as a child-actor in Hollywood, and this movie seemed so entirely unconventional. It was like hippies were making a movie, except George wasn't a hippie. He had his USC letterman jacket on all the time. But it was a film being made by people who loved movies as art and as a way of life. They were cinema students and movie buffs and film-lovers.

That's not what I knew. I was used to gaffers who had been in World War II and had tattoos of anchors on their arms, and sounded like sailors and cowboys. It was a very different environment. Everything that surrounded *American Graffiti* was unconventional. The approach, the way it was shot, the way George dealt with the actors. I fell in love with it. I was fascinated. I was learning every hour of every night that I was there.

One night, 18-year-old Ron and 28-year-old George were standing around Mel's Diner in between setups in San Francisco, getting ready to do a scene. I had been accepted to USC Film School, and I knew that he was a legend there already, so I asked him what he was thinking of doing next. George told me he wanted to use the special effects that Stanley Kubrick introduced in *2001: A Space Odyssey* (1968) and do a kind of *Flash Gordon* movie—like the old serial movies— and he wanted it to be sci-fi and have things that moved fast instead of slow. That was all he really said about it, except that he wanted an entire universe, with lots of aliens. It was about a one-minute description of what would one day be *Star Wars*. I thought he was nuts! It sounded like the craziest idea and the most difficult thing imaginable. But there it was. If I'd really been paying attention, I would have known all about it.

How did it feel when it came to fruition?

I knew he was making *Star Wars*, and I knew that was the movie that he'd been talking about out in front of Mel's Diner, but I had heard all kinds of crazy stories about it from people who'd read the script. However, when I read so much about *Star Wars* in the press, I knew it was a big deal. I didn't see any early screenings, and I hadn't really even talked to George about it, but my wife, Cheryl, and I went to the movie opening day at the then Grauman's Chinese Theatre in Hollywood. I had so much anticipation because I'd read a lot of interesting things about it and I already felt a connection with George...and the movie just completely blew our minds. It transported us; it moved us. It was wildly entertaining. It was really a new dimension of film-making.

We'd stood in line for about two hours to get into the screening, and when we left there were already two huge lines formed for the next couple of screenings. All we did was ask each other if we wanted to see it again, and the answer was yes. And practically without words, because we were so blown away, we just went and got into another two-hour line, and waited, and saw the movie again that day.

Did *Star Wars* inspire you as a filmmaker?

It inspired me as a film-lover. As a filmmaker, at that point, I was already committed to making short films, but I was just about to make my first Roger Corman movie as a director. It was so intimidating and I really ▸

2 /

1 / An iconic director takes the helm of the equally iconic *Millennium Falcon* for the latest *Star Wars* adventure. (See previous page)

2 / Behind the scenes on filming the spectacular conveyex chase sequence, complete with a squadron of range troopers.

3 / The boss is pleased! Ron Howard gives his cast the thumbs up after another successful shoot. (See opposite page)

4 / Chewbacca actor Joonas Suotamo takes direction on set. (See opposite page)

▶ couldn't quite grasp how it was done. So *Star Wars* inspired me as a lover of cinema, but it was so far beyond what I imagined I could really understand and do as a director. But it certainly made me dream.

Later, when I had a chance to work for George and make *Willow*, I felt that it was like getting my doctorate. I'd made movies; I'd had success. I understood the medium and I had more confidence than ever before, but there was something about tackling that sort of canvas under George's guidance that was really defining for me, and liberating, because it was a big confidence builder. The things that worked and the things that I questioned were all monumental learning experiences.

How does it feel to make a *Star Wars* movie?
This was a huge challenge and an exciting opportunity. I'm grateful for all the past experiences that I've had working in film because the confidence that comes with that allowed me to concentrate on working with the producers and the writers to realize this exciting story.

> ## " It's not exactly an origin story; it's more an early rite of passage. "

As a fan, I had such anticipation for what the movie would be, and it was great to finally get to see it with the rest of the world.

So why was it a good time to add the Han Solo movie to the *Star Wars* legacy?
There's an expectation now that these universes are going to be opened up to audiences. So, while it's daunting to deal with the iconic status of Harrison Ford, I think it's also exciting to think about what

made Han Solo, Han Solo. To go young, obviously, it had to be cast with a different actor, and Alden has done a great job of embodying the beginnings of who this figure will turn out to be.

What I found most interesting about the story is that by going in-depth and focusing on Han, it's not exactly an origin story; it's more of an early rite of passage that's a defining adventure. And that's what's so brilliant about the Kasdan's script. They've offered a stand-alone adventure that is not only very *Star Wars*, it's also a lot of fun, makes sense, and is rewarding. It hits a lot of those grace notes that fans want. But there are a lot of opportunities to track this emotional, psychological evolution of young Han Solo and understand this as a defining experience. The gauntlet that he goes through is something that sends him on the road to being the Han Solo that we're more familiar with.

What is the theme of the film?
Although I wouldn't say that our Han Solo entirely comes to terms with himself yet in this film, I would say it's about facing the gray areas in our lives. It is understanding that you can try to define yourself, but there's some essence that is going to guide you. Even somebody who aspires to be an outlaw is going to be forced to define him or herself through moral choices, and they are going to be defined by those choices, not by the labels they necessarily want to put upon themselves.

Does this film reflect the spirit of the original trilogy of movies?
It very much reflects the spirit of the original movies in the combination of playfulness and thematic focus, mixed with great action and a universe that is fascinating, inviting, entertaining, and a little bit thought-provoking. The script is pretty remarkable in the way that it understands and utilizes the tone of the universe and the movies that we've seen and enjoyed before. In a way, I think this is the first real character study in the galaxy so far for fans. And for me, as somebody who thinks of himself as an actor's director, it was very exciting opportunity. ▶

> "
> # It's very important to actually, finally understand that Han is an orphan. [And] orphans are paradoxes.
> "

▶ What is Han's character? How would you describe him? When I talked to Harrison Ford about it, he said it's very important to actually, finally understand that Han is an orphan. Orphans are paradoxes; they're both needy and selfish. They're bold and fearless at times, yet they also can be frightened and confused by some things, especially human connection and emotional issues. It was really interesting to have a chat with Harrison, who's such a thoughtful actor, about what he feels makes Han tick. Those are some of the ideas that he underlined that I think Larry and Jon Kasdan also understand as well. I think the moments are there to reflect that in a very entertaining, non-self-conscious, unpretentious way. But true to *Star Wars*, thematically, those ideas are there along with all the fun, swashbuckling and action.

Why do you think Han and Chewie as a pair have such enduring appeal?
There's a simple nobility and kind of clarity to Chewie. Not only is he an important co-pilot and a powerful figure to have in the trenches with you because of his terrorizing physical presence, but he does also have a conscience. And although Han learns from a lot of characters in this movie and those relationships help define who he's going to be a decade or so later, it is that quiet, barely articulated but fully demonstrated nobility that Han learns from Chewie. At the same time, Chewbacca can be terrified of things and have a horrible temper, and really needs to learn to chill. So, the fact that Han won't take him too seriously, or allow him to take himself too seriously, is probably a good thing for Chewie. He needs that.

How have you found working with the crew?
I like British crews. I've made a lot of movies in London and all over Europe with largely British crews. It's one of the epicenters of the medium. The talent in front of and behind the camera is spectacular. There you've got the crème de la crème. There's a joy and a thrill for me, and an acknowledgement, even, that when the hours get long and the challenges are pretty daunting, I can feel that every department head and the team under him or her feels as if they have a responsibility to live up to audiences' expectations, and probably their own expectations, of what a *Star Wars* movie should be. Kathy Kennedy did a great job

creating an environment where everybody's expected to be 100-percent professional, prepared and ready to work hard, and they're respected for that. Kathy loves films, and she loves *Star Wars*. I think she expects that of other people too. Others rise to that standard very quickly and with real commitment. So, it was exciting to be around.

Many of the crew's parents, and even grandparents, worked on the original movies. How did that continuity help you as a director?
It certainly helped me because, while I've loved the movies, I'm not encyclopedic on the subject. So here I am directing the movie, but constantly looking to people to ask if this creative idea that I have belongs in the *Star Wars* galaxy. So the fact that there's an innate cultural understanding from people who've loved the movies themselves, or whose parents worked on projects before they did, is incredibly helpful. But here's what I respect the most: when I go on the sets of some television productions or even other film franchises, I feel like there's almost a wry devaluation of it all, because it has all been done before. I didn't feel that for one minute of one hour of any day on set. I felt people were striving for excellence within the framework of what that means in the *Star Wars* universe. It was not only exciting, but exciting to be around. I'd like to acknowledge that, and I took a lot of energy from that. It was great. ●

5 / Chewbacca takes a moment to enjoy the breathtaking scenery.

6 / Emilia Clarke and Alden Ehrenreich prepare to take a landspeeder for a spin. (See opposite page)

7 / Writer Lawrence Kasdan and Ron Howard discuss bringing a screen icon to life.

5 /

↓Ξ∇I □∏↓∇I∏↓

THE KASDANS STRIKE BACK

Who better to delve into the early misadventures of Han Solo than the man who penned *The Empire Strikes Back* and *Return of the Jedi*, Lawrence Kasdan? Only this time, he's keeping it in the family by co-writing *Solo* with his son, Jonathan Kasdan. Overseeing it all was producer and Lucasfilm president Kathleen Kennedy.

What are your thoughts on the character of Han Solo?

Kathleen Kennedy (producer): He's very authentic. He's a scoundrel, he's a maverick, and there's a sense of mystery about him. Handsome, incredibly charismatic, and adorable—that's a pretty great combination for a *Star Wars* action hero.

When George Lucas outlined his plans to you for standalone *Star Wars* stories, *Solo* was one of the first he suggested. What made you both want to approach Lawrence Kasdan to write it?

KK: Larry Kasdan knows Han Solo better than anybody. Given his long association with *Star Wars*, and deep understanding of Han Solo's character, there was no one better to tell the story, and preserve the spirit and feeling of the original movies.

Lawrence, what made you want to return to the world of *Star Wars*, and Han Solo specifically?

Lawrence Kasdan (writer): Han was always my favorite, right from the start. He's the most exciting guy in the saga for me. He's unpredictable. He's reckless. He's not particularly brilliant. He'll say things that he can't back up. He'll leap in when he should stay back. There's nothing more attractive to me than a screw-up who's actually got a good heart but hides it as best he can.

The introduction of Han Solo in *Star Wars: A New Hope* was your primary inspiration for his backstory in *Solo*. Why was that?

LK: I've made two Westerns, and there's nothing more Western than the Mos Eisley cantina in *A New Hope*. In walks the gunfighter—he looks like a gunfighter, he sits like a gunfighter, he shoots like a gunfighter—and I thought, *What happened before this guy walked in the door?*

Jonathan, you grew up with *Star Wars* and you're also a fan. Given your love of the saga, how did you approach co-writing *Solo*?

Jonathan Kasdan (writer): I come at this as a fan who thinks of these stories as written in stone, while Larry comes at it as a dramatist who thinks of them as tools. Because I'm more of a *Star Wars* geek than he will ever be, it formed a dynamic between us which determined how much of the lore we were going to be beholden to and how much we were going to go our own way. I think that my reverence and Larry's confidence complemented each other well in the writing process.

You were on set during the entire production of *Solo*. What did you think when you saw Alden Ehrenreich bring a young Han Solo to life?

JK: Han is confident and funny, yet self-conscious and relatable. Alden is perfect in the role, and it was a marvel watching him perform.

1 / Jonathan and Lawrence Kasdan observe the action on set. The father and son team's distinctive styles complemented each other in the writing process, according to Jonathan. (See previous page)

2 / Han Solo and Chewbacca at the start of their friendship.

"
[Han Solo] is the most exciting guy in the saga for me. He's unpredictable.
"
- Lawrence Kasdan

Did you enjoy writing for Han and Chewie again?
LK: I love that relationship. I love all the qualities that are embodied by it. There's courage, there's teamwork, there's loyalty, and there's a slightly canted view of the world. Their relationship is reassuring, recognizable, and speaks to the best in each of them.

Why do you think Han and Chewie's dynamic works so well?
JK: It's a great partnership. It's loaded with love. It's never cruel or hostile, there's a real intimacy.

It feels as though you wanted *Solo* to be the most character-filled and character-focused story yet, but one that still honors the legacy of the saga...
LK: This is a story that comes out of old-time storytelling. It's a story about someone being forged in the crucible of life—in danger, in violence, and in love. It's about how a person is formed. Other people will judge if we succeeded. But for me, that part has been totally achieved. ●

⎯⎯⎯⎯⎯⎯⎯⎯⎯⎯⎯⎯⎯⎯

A NEW ORDER

THE STORY SO FAR....

As the Empire rises, the inhabitants of the galaxy struggle against the tyranny of the new regime.

The galaxy is in the midst of dark days. With the fall of the Republic, the Empire has risen and continues to expand—exhibiting its might and increasing its stranglehold on every planet throughout the system. In the process, Emperor Palpatine and his acolytes lay claim to everything of worth which will help them achieve their goal of ongoing growth.

When Grand Moff Tarkin decrees that all regional governors must increase production in the factories, mines and shipyards within their sectors to help fuel the Imperial war machine, the results are felt far and wide. Imperial presence increases on Corellia and the Empire takes control of the long-established and highly regarded ship yards, allowing the world to continue its slide into poverty. Meanwhile, the planet of Mimban remains in a trench war conflict as the Mimbanese revolt against the Imperial off-worlders who exploit their mining interests.

On Kessel, the royal family allows one half of the planet to be taken over by mining operations, opening the doorway to a notorious criminal gang in the process, while Vandor, a stunning if somewhat inhospitable frontier world, becomes home to a secluded, high-security Imperial vault. Only the far-flung Savareen, a popular destination for smugglers owing to the planet's undocumented shadowport, remains relatively untouched by the Empire.

However, as the Empire expands into the lawless Outer Rim Territories it begins to encounter the criminal gangs who have long ruled there—including the notorious Pyke Syndicate and the newly emerging Crimson Dawn. It is against this backdrop of treachery, corruption and oppression that one young man from Corellia fights for survival against seemingly impossible odds, and nurtures his dreams of a better life. ●

FLYBOYS &
SCOUNDRELS
LIVING ON THE EDGE

As the Empire tightens its iron grip on the galaxy, never has a life in the shadows seemed more appealing. Outlaws and smugglers choose to take their chances, and run the risk of incurring Imperial wrath...

HAN SOLO
THE KID FROM CORELLIA

From a street urchin in the slums of Corellia to hotshot smuggler by way of the Empire, Han Solo has one goal: to become the best pilot in the galaxy.

It is a dark time in the galaxy and Han Solo, born during the dying years of the Republic, has grown up under the oppressive rule of the Galactic Empire on the planet Corellia. Once a rich, proud, sea-faring nation renowned for its ship-building throughout the galaxy, Corellia has fallen upon hard times since the Imperial occupation and the blue-collar planet has been reduced to near-poverty. Under Imperial rule, construction has been ramped up—but while the rich get richer, the poor get poorer and numerous slums pepper the cities. Those who don't work for the Empire are often forced into thievery to survive, and it is in these circumstances that the young Han Solo spends the early years of his life.

Although he reveals little of his childhood, Han has been running scams on the streets since he was 10 years old, and as a teenager he joins one of Corellia's most notorious black-market gangs—the White Worms. Cocky, daring and resilient, Han is a capable fighter – which makes him valuable to the gang. Han carries a pair of aurodium-plated chance cubes with him for luck.

Despite his bleak situation, Han holds on to his ambitions of becoming a world-class pilot—the best in the galaxy—and in a desperate bid to escape Corellia and achieve his dream, enrols in the Imperial Academy on Carida—despite his feelings towards the Empire. However, his roguish character and lack of respect for authority soon sets him at odds with the strict military regime, and despite exhibiting exceptional piloting skills during his time with the academy, they're not enough to save him from being moved to the infantry division when he makes one reckless move too many. He eventually finds himself reassigned from the flight academy to the Imperial Army—serving as a mudtrooper on the war-torn planet of Mimban.

It's during his time on Mimban that Han encounters Beckett and his gang for the first time—and makes an important new acquaintance when he rescues a captured Wookiee from Imperial Camp Forward. When Han gets the chance to join Beckett and his crew of outlaws as part of a heist, it's the opportunity he has been waiting for his whole life and he seizes it with both hands. With his trusty gunslinger's belt and holster at his side, Han leaves the employ of the Empire for good.

With a reckless disregard for common sense, Han lives on trusting his instincts—but it's a gamble that doesn't always pay off. He makes the ultimate gamble when he embarks on a fateful round of sabacc with galaxy-famous gambler and scoundrel, Lando Calrissian. The stakes of the game? Calrissian's customized freighter, which goes by the name of the *Millennium Falcon*.... ●

ALDEN EHRENREICH

The actor who plays Han Solo on playing the title role in *Solo: A Star Wars Story*.

How did you feel when you landed the role of one of the most iconic and best loved movie characters?
When I got the role, I was over the moon—I was ecstatic! It's really special to be part of a franchise that has so much heart and that means so much to people. I loved the way that Lucasfilm were doing it. I loved the humor of the story and their take on the character.

We learn a lot about Han's early life in this film, including the people who helped shape his personality. Can you tell us about some of these people?
The relationship that Han has with Beckett is very important to him. Ultimately he learns how much he wants to be like this guy, and also how he wants to be different, which is true of meeting people who you admire and then getting to know them. [Then there's] Qi'ra, who is a dynamic character with a lot of mystery. You don't quite know what's going on with her, and neither does Han, and that's what keeps the tension going.

What was it like working with the actors who played Beckett and Qi'ra?
Woody Harrelson is such a great actor, and a phenomenal guy. He is just perfect for this role—Woody has that kind of edge that makes Beckett so interesting. Emilia Clarke is just phenomenal and really did a great job with the role. She's very compelling to watch, and very funny. She has a great sense of humor, and our banter in the movie is really wonderful.

The film also features characters who fans are already familiar with—Chewbacca and Lando Calrissian.... How are they portrayed in *Solo*?
Chewie and Han's relationship is really fun to watch because they act like an old married couple. But Chewie also has qualities that are like a dog: he's emotional and loyal—he really cares about Han.
When you meet Lando in the original movies, he's

kind of a reformed guy. In this film, he's still a freewheeling, outlaw pilot. You see a lot more of his style, a lot more of his ship, a lot more of his capes. You see what he and his world were like before you met Lando in the original movies.

What role does Lando play in young Han's life?
Lando is a great foil for Han because they have a lot in common in terms of competitiveness, and the way they interact is really fun. It's complicated with them. That competitive streak only increases when they are up against each other. What you get to see over the course of the film is how two alpha guys, who are each trying to be the fastest pilot and the fastest cowboy and the coolest guy in the room, end up having a grudging respect and understanding and affection for each other.

Donald [Glover] brings a ton of humor and a lot of heart to the film. What you get to see are more emotional moments, more vulnerable moments with him. It was really fun doing those scenes with Donald.

> **"There's a quick-shooting cowboy quality to everything that gives it a slightly different edge and a cooler vibe for *Star Wars*."**

How does the tone of *Solo* compare to the other *Star Wars* movies?
This movie has a toughness to it in a way that is different from the idealism of the Jedi. There's a quick-shooting cowboy quality to everything that gives it a slightly different edge and a cooler vibe for *Star Wars*. As a kid I loved the cantina and all the underground figures with people pulling guns on each other—like a western. This movie is an expansion of that kind of world. There are crime organizations, fancy ones and low-end ones, and denizens of the underworld.

How would you sum up the movie?
It's really funny and very exciting, not to mention a great adventure story on par with movies like *The Adventures of Robin Hood* (1938). You see a lot of different worlds and environments, and you meet a ton of new characters. Plus, there are a lot of thrilling action sequences on top of it all. ●

2 /

3 /

4 /

1 / Alden Ehrenreich as
Han Solo. (See previous
spread)

2 / Han attempts to
negotiate his way out
of trouble.

3 / Confronting Enfys Nest.

4 / Keeping his cool in
the face of danger.

5 / Han takes aim—and
strikes a familiar pose!

7 /

6 / Han arrives to meet with Lando. (See opposite page)

7 / A winning hand? Han looks confident but...

8 / Lando easily matches opponent's swagger!

8 /

11 /

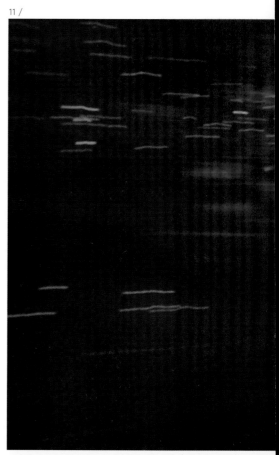

THE KESSEL RUN

While working with Beckett and his gang, Han set a legendary record for making the Kessel Run—a notoriously difficult flight route—in just 12 parsecs. Owing to its perilous position close to the constantly shifting Si'Klaata Cluster and the Akkadese Maelstrom, the space around Kessel is full of treacherous obstacles such as ice chunks, naturally occurring gravity wells and other general debris which make hyperspace travel particularly hazardous. The traditional routes away from the planet are slow but relatively safe, traversing the most stable parts of space. However, avoiding these and skipping through shifting gaps instead can reduce the runtime significantly. However, the challenges are great, and only the extremely brave—or the extremely foolhardy—ever attempt it. Han is never one to embrace the safe option, and the *Millennium Falcon* soon finds itself facing possibly its greatest test to date. ●

10 /

12 /

ᒑᗡᗡ∧ᒃ∨ ∨ᒃᗡᒑᒃᙁᗡ

CHEWBACCA
THE LOYAL SIDEKICK

Delivered from a desolate Imperial imprisonment by Han Solo
and a group of outlaws, the honorable Wookiee
becomes an unexpected ally.

Betrayed, broken and abandoned far from his homeworld, Chewbacca the Wookiee cuts a desperate—but still fearsome —figure when Han Solo rescues him from his mud-soaked prison in Mimban's Camp Forward. Little does he know that that this fateful meeting will be the start of a life-long friendship.

Originally from the forest world Kashyyyk, Chewbacca fell victim to the Empire's drive for slave labor when Imperial troops landed on the planet and broke tribes and families apart, deporting the Wookiees —renowned for their strength—to be used in Empire labor camps throughout the galaxy. Although Chewie managed to escape, he found himself a fugitive on the run and consequently ended up imprisoned on Mimban, where Imperial troops nicknamed him "The Beast," and kept him shackled and starved in an abandoned ammo dump.

In his 190 (standard) years Chewbacca has seen a lot, but following his rescue, rather than directly heading for home, the brave Wookiee remains loyally by Han's side. He joins Solo when he is recruited to Beckett's gang, following him from the snow-capped frontier world of Vandor (where he endures a particularly hair-raising adventure on the roof of a rapidly moving conveyex) to the depths of space aboard the *Millennium Falcon*.

Toting a scattershot blaster rifle and bedecked in heavy flight goggles and what will become his trademark ammo harness (a substitute for his original Wookiee bowcaster and bandolier), Chewbacca's towering, fur-covered build is instantly recognizable. The fact his imposing appearance is enough to strike fear into the heart of even the staunchest underworld villain isn't a bad thing, considering the company Han often keeps.

The Wookiee becomes the would-be smuggler's closest confidant and the pair soon establish an easy rapport and close bond. Despite their wildly differing approaches to life—Chewbacca's older, wiser, and calmer temperament is almost a complete contrast to Han's sometimes arrogant and often-wreckless attitude—the unlikely comrades make a formidable team, with the mature Wookiee often acting as the voice (or growl) of reason in response to his younger friend's sometimes hot-headed decisions.

And so it is that Chewbacca embarks on a life of adventure that will see him travel the galaxy with Han and become co-pilot of the *Millennium Falcon*.... ☺

1 /

2 /

4 /

1 / Han and Chewie where they belong: piloting the *Millennium Falcon*. (See opposite page)

2 / Chewie says a respectful farewell. (See opposite page)

3 / Ready to play holochess against a brave competitor.

4 / Han and Chewie on Savareen.

5 / Man and Wookiee— friends for life.

6 / Chewie transports the spoils of the raid.

7 / Han and Chewie hang on for dear life as they ride the Imperial conveyex! (See following page)

5 /

6 /

3 /

ᔭᎧᎧᏉᎡᏦᎩ ᎡᏞᎧᎧᏉᏦᏟᎧ

CHEWBACCA
AND THE CREATURES

Neal Scanlan, twice Academy Award-nominated for his creature work on The Last Jedi and The Force Awakens, is once again responsible for populating the Solo environments with an extraordinary array of creatures. Scanlan and his talented team produced more than 500 designs for the creatures during the design process.

Why was it important to look back at creature designs from the original trilogy as part of the creation process for this film?

Neal Scanlan (special effects and makeup): I can imagine the conversations George Lucas would have had looking at the films that inspired *A New Hope*—films like *Buck Rogers* and *Flash Gordon*, and encouraging his crew to use those references as inspiration, and push forward in time to find a new and unique version of that world.

For me, it was looking at those worlds, the styles and approaches used, which made them new and fresh for the audiences then, and try to bring some of that into this project. We needed to be observant of *Star Wars*. There is a great deal of charm and innocence to those designs, and some of the simplest creations happen to also be the most unearthly. That's where we have tried to base our designs for this film.

The design of the creatures in the various environments reflects the tone of the settings. Was that a conscious decision?

When one tries to set up a mood, everything needs to fit within that mood—otherwise, it's going to jar. We start this film in a world that's quite dark—a repressed environment—and the creatures we have designed for these environments are not dissimilar. But the film brightens as it goes on, mostly because of the growing relationship between Han and Chewbacca, which is at the very core of what this film is about. Ultimately it's about finding the one being in the world Han can absolutely trust—and it happens to be this Wookiee named Chewbacca.

How did you achieve the 'savage' Chewbacca look?

We were so precious about being accurate and honoring the original Chewbacca suit, that the idea of throwing mud all over him and wetting him down seemed abusive. We got the hose out and literally doused Chewbacca down, and something magical happened—It made him immediately feral. He took on that sorrowful, bedraggled look, just like a domestic dog.

It was interesting to see how quickly these animal qualities came out... and the whole premise is that he looks really animalistic: the beast of Mimban! He's been in prison for some time, he's covered in mud, and he appears first as a shape in the shadows. That's a terrifying experience for Han. ▶

There are Wookiee slaves in the Kessel scenes. Why did you use a cast of the original Chewbacca mask to build these?

Chewbacca is the stud Wookiee, and all things come from him. I think the Wookiees look very successful for that reason. You still see Chewbacca in there somewhere, and that gives all the Wookiees a soul and an acceptability that they are part of this race. I think that is crucially important to making them work as men in suits.

Your team referenced Indian deities like Kali to inspire the design of Rio Durant. What was the thought process?

We started to sketch ideas of what he might look like. To have arms that emanate from the shoulders, with the dexterity of a monkey, enabling him to swing and work as well upside down as he can the right way. And he can use his feet as well as his hands. It's very important to retain the humanity of a character visually, and create a design that is endearing, not intimidating, to appeal to an entire age range.

1 / Chewbacca stays warm on Vandor. (See previous spread)

2 / Wookiees flank Tak (Anthony Daniels) during the revolution on Kessel.

3 / "The Beast" Chewbacca gets a firm grip on a surprised Han Solo. (See opposite page)

CREATING CHEWIE

How to build a Wookiee...

The creature effects department produced eight Chewbacca suits and ten Chewbacca heads.

The same supervising animatronics designer, Maria Cork, has worked with Chewbacca since 2015's *The Force Awakens*.

Chewbacca's suit consists of a Lycra under-suit with a knitted cowl. This is a more modern material—the original was completely knitted in wool by original *Star Wars* makeup artist Kathleen Freeborn.

Chewbacca's hair is exactly the same as the original suit, and is made of singular knotted hairs of yak and mohair.

Cleaning the suit every day wasn't possible, so the crew created a "Wookiee Wash" on set—a big shower unit rigged above a paddling pool.

► How did you approach the design of Lady Proxima, Moloch, and the White Worms...

We tried a lot of designs for both Lady Proxima and Moloch. We felt that Moloch and the White Worm aides all had to be derivative of Lady Proxima, so it was important to get that design locked first. The idea is that Lady Proxima is almost interconnected to her aides—similar to a tree's root system, by which she feeds them nutrients and but also passes on information to them. At some point Moloch would have broken free, become an independent entity, but he is telepathically and almost physically connected to her in many ways.

The creatures at the sabacc game were inspired by a Caravaggio painting. What was the thinking there?

It's a beautiful painting, an incredible composition, and it has a great atmosphere to it. The characters sit round a table and many of them fall into the background shadows. We substituted the humans for aliens at the same proportions as in the painting. The filmmakers chose the creatures they liked from a catalog of creatures we were already drawing at concept stage, and we pulled the ones that were most favorable, not only because of the way they looked, but because their proportions fitted the frame.

5 /

4 / Moloch confronts a stormtrooper on Corellia.

5 / The Caravaggio-inspired sabacc game.

6 / A gambler tries his luck at sabacc.

6 /

7 /   8 /

7 / Background dwellers in
the Lodge at Fort Ypso.

8 / Margo, Dryden Vos'
concierge who looks after
the guests aboard the
First Light.

9 / The all-seeing Six Eyes.
(See opposite page)

Six Eyes, an alien player in the sabacc game, has the most sophisticated mechanical head ever produced. He has 50 servos inside the head, with on-board intelligence. How does that work?

As the puppeteer moves around inside, the eyes automatically follow, they'll look up, look down, the head will bounce, and the eyes will bounce. All of that can be done before the director starts to suggest movement. The sabacc game, essentially a poker game, was a perfect place for a character like this. Six Eyes has the ability to look at anyone's cards at any one time, and the other players don't know which eye is looking at them! ●

QI'RA

THE LAWBREAKER

With a talent for criminal brilliance, how far can Qi'ra really be trusted?

As a human Corellian living in the slums of Coronet, Qi'ra was once part of the notorious gang known as the White Worms. Thieving and scamming on the city streets alongside a young rogue named Han, she conspired to procure items to sell on the planet's black market. By the age of 18, Qi'ra had used her cunning and intelligence to work her way up to the position of Head Girl among the scrumrats, having come to the attention of Lady Proxima—the matriarch of the gang—after negotiating a particularly profitable deal. Although the matriarch respected the opinion of her Head Girl, she stopped short of trusting her, believing that Qi'ra would eventually use her natural talents to scheme against her. After the young criminal eventually broke free of the gang and escaped the slums of Corellia, she subsequently fell in with the crime syndicate known as Crimson Dawn.

When Han Solo is reunited with Qi'ra on board the Crimson Dawn's yacht, the *First Light*, several year later, the cool and calculating woman who stands before him is a far cry from the street smart young urchin that he worked alongside as a scrumrat in Coronet. Since escaping that life of drudgery, Qi'ra climbed her way through the ranks of Crimson Dawn, until she came to the attention of Dryden Vos. The crime lord was impressed by the young woman and made her his trusted lieutenant; he now grooms her to take on the projects he is unable to manage and she has become extremely influential.

Her designer outfits are a long way from the rags she wore on Corellia and serve as a convincing disguise to hide her poverty-ridden past. Now, responsible for organizing Vos' schedule and managing the servants and events on board the ship, Qi'ra's strength as a strategist have come to the fore. She negotiates trade deals with business associates and is responsible for making numerous high-powered decisions, but her skills go beyond the meeting rooms of the *First Light*. Trained to fight by Dryden Vos, Qi'ra is an accomplished practitioner of Teräs Käsi and adept with a blaster. All of these traits, combined with her ability to obtain a variety of objects through her Crimson Dawn contacts, make her an extremely useful ally, but an equally dangerous adversary for anyone who crosses her. ●

2 /

EMILIA CLARKE

The actress best-known for her work on *Game of Thrones* plays the savvy Qi'ra

What made you want to get involved with this film?
The Force Awakens was such an incredible piece of work and so stunning. The *Star Wars* universe has been given a whole new makeover, and an opportunity to be part of that was too good to miss.

What draws your character Qi'ra to Han?
Han and Qi'ra grew up together and were incredibly close when they were younger. Han is an opportunist, and even if he doesn't know what he's doing, he does it anyway! He is incredibly endearing and he always lands on his feet. He does these stupid things that should never work, but they do, which is impressive! And he does it all with bravado. It's satisfying to him.

Why have Han and Chewie become such enduring and loved characters?
When they find each other, Han and Chewie are lost souls, and they become the epitome of friends forever. They have each other's back. It's the ultimate bromance. ▶

1 / Emilia Clarke as Qi'ra. (See previous page)

2 / Qi'ra and her prisoner. But things are not all they seem...

3 / Qi'ra, a woman not to be crossed.

4 / At her most glamorous with Han. (See opposite page)

5 / Enjoying Lando's wardrobe aboard the *Millennium Falcon*. (See opposite page)

▶ What do you think Alden brings to the character of Han Solo?

He is an incredible actor, who did this role justice. He is also one of the hardest workers I've ever seen. The amount of work that he's put into this role is staggering, and it shows. He brings that Han Solo swagger. He's got an endearing quality about him, as a person, and he really brings it to this movie.

> "
> ## It's been really fun to play a new character who is so important to Han. I did a lot of research and geeked up on a lot of stuff...
> "

What did Ron Howard contribute to the film?

Ron was incredible, such a joy to work with. He was like a kid while making this movie—he just loved it. I remember one of the first days on set when he asked Alden if he could see his gun—then he started shooting it! Ron has so much energy. He's really inspiring. He also knows how to sculpt a story. It's his job to mold this story into something that has a beginning, a middle, and an end. He has a great relationship with the writers, Jonathan and Larry Kasdan, and George Lucas and Ron go way back. Ron knows these movies, and he is respectful of them.

Would you say that Ron really gets the characters as well as the spectacle?

Ron really gets the characters, and he gets the relationships between the characters, which is so important because this is what this entire movie is based on. I think that Ron understands that and is sensitive to it, and he deals with those relationships on screen really well. You've got the friendships, you've got a bit of father-son, you've got a bit of love—you've got it all.

How does it feel to be creating such an intriguing new character?

It's really exciting! As someone who has taken on characters that already exist, which can be really daunting and scary, it's been really fun to play a new character who is so important to Han. I did a lot of research and geeked up on a lot of stuff because I wanted to get it right. ●

6 / Qi'ra in action as a skirmish turns nasty.

ꓚꓛꓤꓤꓤꓤ

LANDO CALRISSIAN
CHARM PERSONIFIED

With a winning smile, sparkling repartee, and daring nature, Lando Calrissian's reputation precedes him wherever he goes.

Captain of the *Millennium Falcon*, the retired smuggler, Lando Calrissian, is as cool and sophisticated as they come. A smooth-talking man from Socorro, Lando has the accolade of outwitting and evading the Empire on a number of occasions and is always happy to regale an audience with tales of his exploits. His travels have taken him to the furthest corners of the galaxy, from the Rafa system to Felucia, and his adventures as a daring con-man are almost legendary.

Bedecked in gold jewelry and fine, exotic clothes, Lando is a seemingly successful figure at the sabacc gaming tables on Vandor, where he first encounters would-be smuggler, Han Solo. Flushed with the success of his latest run, he has made enough profit even at his young age to be able to consider quitting the smuggling trade in favor of taking up gambling professionally. For those who know the enigmatic pilot it's an unsurprising career progression, considering that along with flying and smuggling, gambling is one of the great passions in his life. Lando has studied more than 80 variants of sabacc—and knows how to play (and cheat) in all of them. When Han comes in search of the fabled captain, looking for a ship to use as part of a heist, Lando is enjoying some downtime taking stock of his career to date and toying with the idea of chronicling his adventures in a

series of memoirs. However, the potent mix of sabacc and the allure of a profitable job soon prove to be too much and the debonair pilot becomes involved with Beckett and his carefully recruited gang, proudly showing them his ship, the *Millennium Falcon*.

Lando is a connoisseur of beautiful things—and his love of finery extends from the customization of his unique Corellian-built freighter all the way through to his exquisite clothes. A dedicated follower of fashion, he stores his garments in a bespoke walk-in closet adjacent to his living quarters on board the *Falcon*—no doubt one of his many customizations to the ship. The closet holds a multitude of items including shirts, trousers, scarves, and fantastic shoes that he has purchased during his extensive travels—as well as a range of capes that help to make up his signature style. A lover, not a fighter, Lando gives little thought to practicality when selecting his outfits, always confident that his charm and swagger will be enough to get him out of any situation, without the need for any strenuous physical intervention. That said, the slick captain is particularly handy with a blaster pistol and soon proves himself to be a valuable ally.

Always a high-roller, little does Lando realize just how much this fateful meeting with Han will eventually cost him.... ●

DONALD GLOVER

The multi-talented performer on taking Lando to new heights!

What made you want to take on the role of Lando Calrissian?
Lando is an intriguing character. He was the most intriguing character to me when I was a kid, because you didn't really know if you could trust him when you met him. Sometimes he's a good guy and sometimes he's a bad guy. He's only beholden to himself.

Why do you think Lando has such a lasting appeal with *Star Wars* fans?
People like Lando because it's always nice to meet people in life who have flair and style. I think it's a lot of work to put that much style into your everyday life. You have to really care about things, and it shows that you care about perception in life in a different way. I think there's something about Lando that's really graceful and cool.

Was it daunting, taking on the role, especially since another actor made Lando so iconic?
I wasn't really nervous about taking on the Lando role. He is an iconic character, but I was never going to play him like Billy Dee Williams. I'm not Billy Dee Williams and he isn't me. My take on him is probably way different.

I guess in a way it could be considered daunting, but it never felt that way to me. I was just really excited to play somebody like that, given the chance.

To anyone who may be unfamiliar with Lando Calrissian, how would you describe him?
I would say that he's a very particular person, very prim and proper. He's very smooth; he's very self-assured, and he's the type of person who could be the life of the party if he sees it as being advantageous to him.

And Lando definitely has the best clothes! It was great to wear all those costumes. It was really fun to actually be him, to focus on the character and make something unique. I had a blast being Lando. From the hair to the capes to the boots and the whole style, it felt very comfortable.

1 / Stylish and suave, Lando Calrissian as played by Donald Glover. (See previous page)

2 / He may be a lover, not a fighter, but Lando is handy with a blaster too.

3 / Sitting pretty in the pilot's seat of his beloved *Millennium Falcon.*

4 / Lando aboard his pristine pride and joy. But will it stay that way?
(See opposite page)

5 / Effortlessly cool, even in a blaster fight! (See opposite page)

6 / Lando at the controls of the *Falcon* as it makes the jump to lightspeed. (See opposite page)

▶ And you have a cool ship too—the *Millennium Falcon.* Can you describe how it appears in *Solo*?
The *Falcon* in this film is brand-new, which is really cool to see. In between takes, I would hang out in there. It's such a calming, relaxing ship. It's such a bachelor pad. It's kind of funny, but we've never seen it this nice. It's more of a reflection of Lando than Han, because it is Lando's at this point.

Solo has plenty of lighter moments—why do you think comedy is so important for this story?
Good movies need a release valve, so I think comedy is important. There should be something that feels light when there's darkness in the story.

What new things do we learn about Lando in this movie?
Lando is a pretty hard gambler. He's kind of a maverick who I feel has been running around for a while. It's funny, because when you meet Han in *Star Wars: A New Hope*, you feel like he's been doing his thing longer than Lando. But this movie shows that Lando has been around doing this kind of wheeling and dealing for a little bit longer. We get to see more of his world, and what he's known for.

How would you describe the relationship between Han and Lando in this film?
They don't trust each other, but they have a common goal. They have friends in common, and they have people they care about. They are acquaintances who care about each other, but at the end of the day they are also in competition with one another, which I think is complex, but also very real.

What were your initial impressions of the script when you first read it?
I thought it had a lot of heart and presented a view of why people do things. I felt like it hit the sweet spot of being something that everybody could understand, while also being true to the world—not necessarily our world, but very specific to human nature, which I really liked.

What do you think audiences will make of Alden Ehrenreich as Han Solo?
It's cool to see Alden on screen; he's very charismatic. It's cool to see this character all wide-eyed about the nastiness of the world, and how rough it can be. And he plays it so well. Our actual friendship mirrors the friendship on screen, which is really great. ●

> " I had a blast being Lando. "

7 / Place your bets! Lando plays the odds..

L3-37

A DROID WITH ATTITUDE

A droid like you've never seen before, L3-37 is Lando Calrissian's trusty—if somewhat revolutionary—co-pilot aboard the Millennium Falcon.

An extremely capable droid, L3-37 is a one-of-a-kind unit among mechanicals. The very definition of a self-made droid, L3 is constructed from astromech and protocol droid parts. She has built herself in a unique arrangement which gives her a humanoid shape coupled with speech and movement capabilities far beyond those possessed by regular R-series units.

Her brain is also more complex than regular R-series units, incorporating data from espionage droids and combining it with protocol droid processors as well as customized, start-of-the-art coding. While this brain augmentation has made L3-37 extremely intelligent and given her the ability to quickly calculate complex hyperspace routes, it also provided her with a pronounced self-awareness and consciousness. As a result of this she has evolved as an independent thinker with a somewhat confrontational nature, and has developed a distaste for the oppression of droids throughout the galaxy—revolutionary views that she frequently shares in no uncertain terms with the 'organics' who surround her.

However, despite her feelings, she is a dependable part of the *Millennium Falcon*'s crew, and her ability to directly interface with the freighter's state-of-the-art navicomputer, allowing the ship to achieve unparalleled speeds, makes her invaluable to her partner, Lando Calrissian. ●

2 /

3 /

L3-37

4 /

PHOEBE WALLER-BRIDGE

The British actress on creating a motion-captured marvel

How does it feel to have created a new *Star Wars* character?
It feels incredibly cool. She really leapt off the page when I read the script, and she's incredibly funny and inspiring. The fact that she's a droid makes her even more of an unusual character to play.

What has been your personal favorite moment on the film?
Going into hyperspace felt unbelievably real. We were in the cockpit, and there were screens on the outside. When I pushed the lever, the screens went into hyperspace! There were people shaking the cockpit, so for a second, I really believed I was going into hyperspace. I'm an adult, so I knew it wasn't real, but Donald and I just went "Aaaahhhhhh!" like we were really there.

On a daily level, seeing Chewie inbetween shots walking around and having like a snack, or kicking a stone on the floor and looking bored, never got old. That always cracked me up.

What do we find out about Han Solo in the new movie?
Audiences get to have a little peek into where some of his edge came from. There are some softer sides to his personality that you witness, which is really nice to see, because he's quite a closed character. His roguishness, I think, can sometimes be seen as a distancing from other people—he doesn't seem to want to make connections. And in this film, you do see some connections that he's made, and how they've affected him.

What was it like to work with the creatures in the film?
They usually either have people inside them or they're being puppeteered. It's amazing how quickly chatting to giant slugs becomes normalized! There's something very magical and inclusive about the idea of so many different types of creatures in this film. We had a tour of the creature workshop, and were shown a mechanical lizard head that had around 200 different little muscles in its face. We asked the puppeteer if he could make it do angry and surprised at the same time. And he could! ●

5 /

1 / L3-37, a droid created using motion-capture by actress Phoebe Waller-Bridge. (See previous page)

2 / Lando and his copilot share a lighter moment. (See opposite page)

3 / L3-37 takes the controls as Han and Lando look on.

4 / Lando's droid shares his distinctive style of greeting.

MILLENNIUM FALCON

THE FASTEST SHIP
IN THE GALAXY

The unbridled vision of a daring smuggler and some
much needed tender-loving care transformed this once ordinary
freighter into a sporty, highly covetable starship.

1 /

2 /

3 /

Once upon a time, the *Millennium Falcon* was no more than a Corellian Engineering light-weight freighter, hauling cargos in the busiest spacelanes of the galaxy—but then Lando Calrissian got his hands on it. Seeing through the plain exterior to the powerful engines and well-built Corellian ship underneath, the gambler made it his mission to help the *Falcon* reach its full potential—and after two years of modifications and customization, his goal was eventually realized.

Sleek and sophisticated, Lando imbued the ship with his own impeccable sense of style, both externally and internally. He had the exterior of the ship skinned with a lightweight shell of durasteel, colored in alabaster, with crys-anoblue highlights, and used his imagination to transform the two distinctive cargo mandibles at the front of the vessel into an auxiliary launch instead. Meanwhile, an outrigger cockpit, resplendent with its distinctive window, housed the main controls.

Internally, the ship was restored to pristine condition with slick, gleaming white hallways, a fully fitted crew lounge complete with drinks bar, sofas, sound system and a holochess dejarik table, as well as a luxurious captain's quarters featuring a grooming area, extra-wide bed and a walk-in closet.

Fitted with a heavy laser cannon and a deflector shield generator, and powered by a bank of sublight engines which offered precise control when it came to acceleration and maneuverability, the *Falcon* was a masterpiece of ship-building, but its crowning glory was its hyperdrive system, which Lando's droid co-pilot, L3-37, was able was able to interface with to achieve amazing speeds.

For a smuggler as cool and sophisticated as Lando, the *Falcon* proved to be the perfect ship; capable of transporting deceptively heavy loads thanks to its ample cargo space. The powerful engines and streamlined design helped whenever a quick getaway was necessary —and all while looking effortlessly stylish. ●

1 / The luxurious interior of the ship.

2 / The *Falcon* arrives at the refinery at Savareen.

3 / Docked on Kessel.

4 / The impressive image of the *Millennium Falcon* in flight. (See opposite page)

THE STYLE SHIP

"The *Millennium Falcon* is Lando's really cool bachelor pad, not to mention a great party ship. It has a large living room with an area for drinks and food, as well as a stereo system and gaming station. The bedroom has a huge closet filled with what seems like a million capes. If I were traveling throughout the galaxy, this is definitely the ship I'd want to be in. I can imagine landing somewhere, letting the ramp down, and having people just hang out inside."
- Donald Glover on the *Millennium Falcon*

THE EXTERIOR

The exterior *Millennium Falcon* set built for *The Force Awakens* and *The Last Jedi* was repurposed. Situated on the Pinewood Studios backlot, it weighed 31 tons.
It required two cranes to move the ship. As a result, the *Falcon* could be seen flying across the Buckinghamshire skies on more than one occasion during the Summer months of 2017 as it was repositioned from one space to another for filming.

The exterior was given a smooth outer shell, the missing panels replaced, and the internal pipes and mechanisms covered up.

A wedge-shaped escape pod was placed between the front mandibles.

5 / The full-size *Falcon* on location.

6 / The living quarters of the ship reflect Lando's suave, stylish personality.

7 / A view from the cockpit.

THE INTERIOR

The interior *Millennium Falcon* set took three months to build and is the largest interior *Falcon* set ever made on any Star Wars film.

Filmmakers repurposed elements created for *The Force Awakens* and *The Last Jedi*, expanding the interior to encompass Lando's quarters, which includes an extensive walk-in closet and a luxurious sleeping area, a double bed draped in soft fabrics and surrounded by controls and gadgets to keep Lando entertained—and entertaining! Among other pieces, the set decorating team sourced a pair of square dumbbells and a pair of silver headphones, a nod to a similar pair seen in *A New Hope*, hooked on a seat in the main hold.

The creative team were tasked to add elements to suggest the *Falcon* is a more social place under Lando's guardianship. In the lounge, a chandelier has been added over the familiar chess table, and some yellow protective covers to the seating area. The area now offers a bar, a circular ottoman seat with integral music system and a brand-new navigation system control, which retains some elements of the older version but is a much slicker and well-maintained piece of machinery.

A trophy case, containing Lando's prize possessions, includes a miniature replica of the *Falcon* itself, 3D printed from the working model that was made for the build of the exterior ship, a speeder bike model, as well as a model of Cloud City.

Yellow upholstery throughout is inspired by the color of Lando's shirt.

The engine room was added to the interior set, an area that has only been hinted at in previous *Star Wars* films.

Utmost respect was paid to the original design when it came to revamping the cockpit. All the control panels were completely remade. There are extra switches, but every LED is in exactly the same place as it is in the original films.

The cockpit had to be as practically interactive as possible, so every switch had to work. Plug-in ports on the right-hand side of the cockpit were added with which L3-37 could interact.

Visual effects utilized rear-projection wrapping screens the height of the soundstage 180 degrees round the cockpit so the actors could see and react to pre-prepared animations rendered by ILM of flying and entering hyperspace.

When exposed to extreme turbulence during the film, the special effects team created the movement with a combination of gimbals and purpose-built rigs.

FALCON FACTS

Known affectionately among the crew as "The Falcon Man," Liam Georgensen is the art director responsible for the *Millennium Falcon*. Dominic Tuohy served as special effects supervisor, overseeing turbulent times on the ship, while the incredible hyperspace effects were created by visual effects supervisor Rob Bredow.

What changes did you make to the *Falcon* in order to establish that this was earlier in the timeline?
Liam Georgensen (art director): The padding in the corridors in *A New Hope* is slightly whiter than it is in *The Empire Strikes Back* and *Return of the Jedi*. We took that as a hint that at an earlier time it was a lot whiter, before Han got his hands on it. So it was a much cleaner version of the corridors. We took that idea and applied it to the areas we don't see in the saga films to work some of Lando's character into the ship, as well as tidying up all the exposed wires and making it much more pristine throughout the areas that audiences know.

Why did you decide to show the specific areas of the *Falcon* that appear on screen?
What we're showing is only a tiny part of the inner workings of the ship, perhaps just an area accessible for maintenance and for giving it a little speed boost when needed, but the idea is to hint at the more industrial side of the ship, which later becomes more exposed once Han has had his way with it.

What approach did you take when it came to designing the cockpit?
We were careful with what we did to the cockpit, but there is still an element of Lando about it. We included fresh upholstery on the chair, and a little pop of yellow on the back seats.

How did you create the effect of the *Falcon* experiencing turbulence?
Dominic Tuohy(special effects supervisor): We made it move to look like it's really in trouble. The set was shaking, and we moved it five degrees either way and very violently, which allowed everything on set to vibrate and move creating natural movement. The actors weren't trying to move; physics took over. They're actually trying to hold on!

Why did you decide to use physical rear-projection to simulate movement and hyperspace?
Rob Bredow (visual effects supervisor): We generated the shots in much the same way it is done for a simulator ride in an amusement park to make it as immersive and realistic as possible, not just for our actors but for the camera, and primarily for the audience. It completely changes the character of the lighting on the actor's face so you can actually see hyperspace in Han's face. As Han Solo goes into hyperspace for the first time in the *Millennium Falcon*, it is reflected in his eyes. Those are shots that would be impossible to get without this technology. ●

HONOR AMONG THIEVES
THE RINGLEADER

Beckett and his gang may look like a motley crew at first glance, but in fact, they're masters of their trade—and their trade just so happens to be pulling off the perfect heist.

Led by the crack-shot gunslinger Tobias Beckett, the unlikely team have pulled off numerous risky robberies. They have set their sights on the ultimate prize, planning to steal precious cargo from a moving Imperial conveyex traversing the inhospitable Iridium Mountains on the icy planet Vandor.

It isn't long before Beckett recruits Han Solo and Chewbacca to join the team—although his decision doesn't meet with everyone's approval. ●

TOBIAS BECKETT

An assured—but debt-ridden—human gunslinger from Glee Anselm, the experienced Beckett has earned a living from staging a string of profitable heists. Despite having surrounded himself with people he trusts, he still maintains the philosophy that treachery and betrayal are a part of life—and doesn't hesitate to impress this dogma on the young Han, warning him to watch his back at every turn. Although Beckett remains guarded about his plans for the future, he evidently hopes they will include a peaceful life with his fellow outlaw, Val.

When Han first meets Beckett, the gang leader is working for Crimson Dawn. However, as a professional thief, Beckett is always involved with the unscrupulous and goes wherever he smells profit. He may not always be the most talkative of people, but Beckett is always thinking and working out the angles, and of course, his unrivalled skills with a blaster make him extremely dangerous.

Although his comrades joke about his advancing years and the fact that he has been around the block, Beckett is not someone to mess with—youthful exuberance and tenacity are all well and good, but sometimes they just can't compete with experience. ●

WOODY HARRELSON

The veteran actor on being Beckett, the leader of the gang.

How did you find working with director Ron Howard on *Solo*, and what do you think he brought specifically to this movie?

It was great to work with Ron because he has basically been in this business longer than almost anybody. He is a master of his craft and he knew what he wanted. Ron's enthusiasm on-set was unbridled and infectious. He had a great time and you could really feel it, which helped the rest of us get fired up.

And how about the father and son writing team, Lawrence and Jonathan Kasdan?

Those guys are true masters of their craft. They know this universe better than anybody. Everything dovetails beautifully from this film into the lore established in the earlier films. You see where many things originated from, including how Han and Chewie first met. They created a really phenomenal script. It's such a cool story, with lots of humor and excitement.

How about the work of Bradford Young, the director of photography? What can fans expect from the look of this movie?

What Bradford did is incredible. He made the movie so beautiful, so aesthetically pleasing. When people

> "
> **It's such a cool story, with lots of humor and excitement.**
> "

view this they're obviously going to be interested in the characters, but they're also just going to be knocked out by how the movie looks—I know that for a fact. Bradford is a real artist.

What has it been like working with Alden Ehrenreich as Han Solo, and what do you think he brings to the role?

Alden is a tremendous actor. He's so dedicated. He's a no-nonsense hard worker. He's taken on this role created by a guy who is about as beloved as it gets. Harrison Ford is a great actor, so Alden is stepping into some big shoes. But I could tell right away that this was perfect casting. You have to care about [Han], and Alden has something about him that is magical. You really do like him immediately. Alden nailed it.

What have been your favorite moments, working on this film?

My favorite moments are the scenes where all of us were involved. You've got Donald, Phoebe, Joonas, Emilia, Alden and I cutting up together, and there were some really big laughs. I loved hanging, acting, and laughing with everyone—it's what I will miss most. I couldn't really call it work. ●

RIO DURANT

A long-time criminal collaborator of Beckett's, Ardennian Rio Durant has a history with the Empire as he formerly fought alongside the Republic's army during the Clone Wars. Helping Beckett develop new schemes, Rio puts his military training to good use. A good-natured team member, he also loves to cook up a delicious meal for his fellow outlaws. He's always up for a challenge and enjoys regaling new acquaintances with far-fetched tales of his previous daring exploits. ●

1 / Woody Harrelson as Tobias Beckett. (See previous spread)

2 / Beckett and Val enjoy a fireside chat. (See opposite page)

3 / The nimble Rio Durant shows off his dexterity!

4

VAL

The gang's experienced explosives expert, Val is cool, confident and always prepared to take on even the most physical challenge to pull off a successful job, whether it be squeezing into a narrow mountain crevice or abseiling down a treacherous cliff-face. Val has seen and done a lot, and although friendly and talkative, she's also a very private person. Displaying an in-depth knowledge of electronics and chemistry, she hand-makes her own weapons of choice—devastatingly effective, magnetically affixed baradium bombs. She's suspicious of outsiders and doesn't take too kindly to the arrival of new team members, whom she considers "amateurs."

Her ability to think on her feet and speedily re-evaluate situations makes her a confident, important team member. While she is open to challenges, she won't take unnecessary risks. ●

4 / Thandie Newton as Val—a cool customer.

THANDIE NEWTON

The actress behind Val on playing a tough explosives expert.

What attracted you to the role?
I was initially attracted by the idea of a film devoted to the introduction of Han Solo. And then I was intrigued by the really interesting band of people that he meets on his journey, made up of Woody Harrelson, myself, and a couple of creatures.

Do you feel that this movie has the same sense of fun that _A New Hope_ had?
I think that there's an anarchic glint in Harrison Ford's eye all the time in that film, and that's something which has been instilled in this telling of Han Solo's story. The actor who plays Han in our movie, Alden Ehrenreich, did such a brilliant job of finding the character for himself without doing a copycat impersonation of Harrison Ford. He brought the character to life in such a detailed way, which allows you to then connect it to the Han Solo that you know and love. It honors the original, but it also lifts it to a whole other place.

What does Woody Harrelson bring to the _Star Wars_ universe?
With the way he delivers a line, the way he moves, the way he interprets the character, Woody brings the unexpected to everything that he does. I think sometimes he surprises even himself. He's very free, very instinctive. He's also the best fun and the first person to laugh at himself, which for a massive movie star like him is quite humbling.

You did some of your own stunts. What was it like?
The biggest chunk of work for me was stunt training. Most of my time was spent preparing for the work I then had to do on set. I absolutely loved it. I would go to work initially wondering how I was going to do these action scenes, even though I trained. Now, I feel like I've been to the university of stunts!

> " **I feel like I've been to the university of stunts!** "

What was it like working with Chewbacca?
Chewbacca exists. He is a fully functioning, fully formed creature. Sometimes I would forget that there was someone inside the amazing costume. There was a whole team of people that were just there to groom this huge beast. The actor who plays him, Joonas Suotamo, was very committed to the character. His voice and the way he moves is exactly the Chewbacca you remember from childhood. I think actually being around Chewbacca was probably the time I got most excited, because that, for me, was pure _Star Wars_.

What was it like working with the writers, Lawrence and Jonathan Kasdan?
Obviously, with a father and son there's all that trust and mutual respect. Jonathan brought a modern vibe to the movie, and his father, Lawrence, is one of the monarchs of the action-movie genre.

They're really the root of the movie, from which everything comes. And they were present on set practically every day that I was there.

I think it was really reassuring for everybody because if we had any questions, we were able to ask them directly.

What did you think of your costume and look?
Different actors have different ways into their characters, and for me, the whole look of the character is when I finally feel like the person I'm supposed to be playing. We were all really excited by the ideas for Val, especially the makeup and the hair. It was a collaboration with our fantastic team, but she really looked how I imagined her to look.

Our producer, Allison Shearmur, had amazing instincts, and she was there when we were creating the look for Val. She was really the one who knitted it all together and kept us all on point. ●

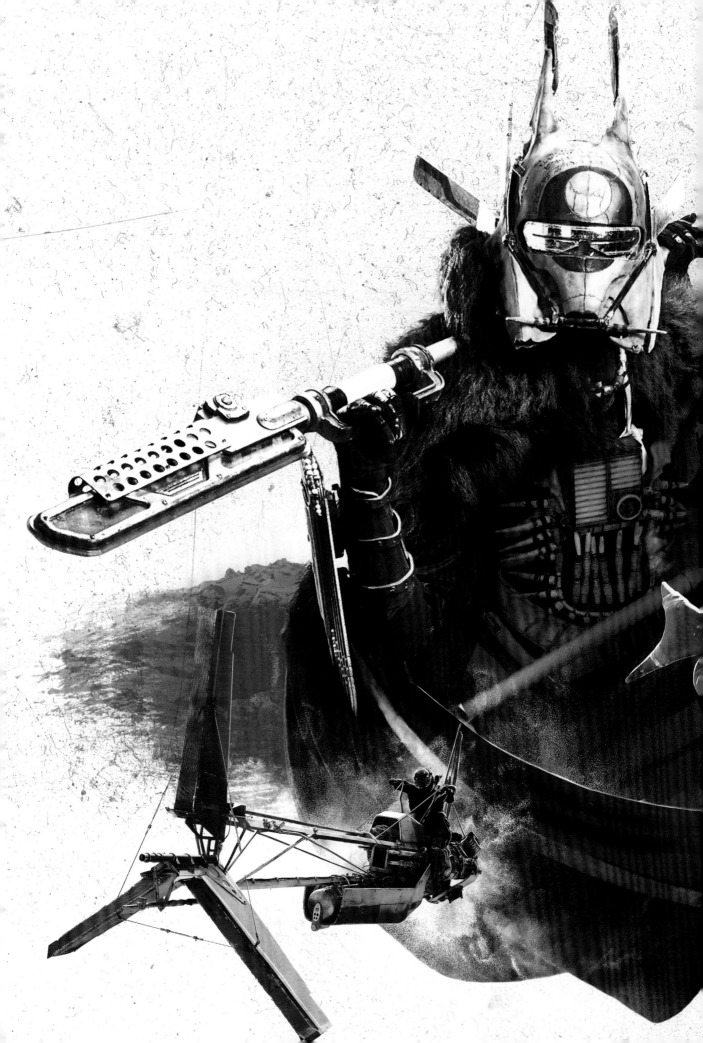

A CRIMINAL ELEMENT
UNDERLORDS OF THE OUTER RIM TERRITORIES

Renowned as the most lawless place in the galaxy, the Outer Rim Territories have long been plagued by various criminal organizations.

ᗡᓓᔑᑎᔿᗀᓓᗡᔑᒪᔑ ᔫᓂᒪᒪᔓᐱᓂᓓᔑ

THE WHITE WORMS

THE CRIMINAL UNDERBELLY OF CORELLIA

In the poverty-stricken city of Coronet, the black market has blossomed, and at its very core is the notorious gang known as the White Worms.

Despite Corellia's faltering economy, the one area that still manages to flourish is crime. Nowhere is that more evident than in the black market of Coronet, where the prevalent gang known as the White Worms continues to facilitate the trade of stolen and prohibited goods, albeit at extremely inflated prices.

Headed up by a water-dwelling Grindalid known as Lady Proxima is an innocuous-looking abandoned water-processing plant in the poorest areas of the city. The plant houses the hidden den of the aquatic matriarch and her subordinates—a small number of fellow Grindalids who 'employ' a team of street urchins known as scrumrats to do their bidding.

The scrumrats are overseen by Lady Proxima's enforcer—Moloch—who considers himself vastly superior to the gang's young humanoid servants. Moloch takes great pleasure in berating and punishing the street urchins—especially the young, smart-mouthed Han.

Although sunlight is dangerous to the Grindalid species, Moloch ventures abroad, protected by heavy, customized armor, and sometimes travels aboard an A-A4B truckspeeder when necessary to negotiate 'business' deals. During such trips he is frequently accompanied by two scrumrat goons named Syke and Rebolt who handle the Corellian hounds (canine-like creatures used in both hunting and for attack).

The scrumrats—child pickpockets, scammers and thieves who make money for Lady Proxima—are at the very bottom of the pile. They are Corellia's unwanted souls, but Proxima exploits their vulnerable state by offering them a meager living working for her. In return, she gives them a rodent-infested area in the sewers of the water-processing plant to call home, where they spend all their time living in almost abject poverty. However, this poverty encourages them to use their initiative and be resourceful in order to survive. Although it's not much, the scrumrats cling to the hope they will be able to impress Proxima enough to one day make the jump to bodyguards like Syke and Rebolt. However, the truth is that very few of the scrumrats impress as much as either Han or Qi'ra, and many live resentfully in their shadows. ●

2 /

3 /

4 /

5 /

1 / Moloch, a sinister figure
in the Corellian underworld.
(See previous spread)

2 / Scrumrats hide out
in the tunnels. (See
opposite page)

3 / Moloch and Han Solo
confer in the sewers
of Corellia.

4 / The foul leader of
the White Worms:
Lady Proxima.

5 / The mastermind behind
the White Worms in all
her glory .

ⴽ ⵀⵍⵓⵠⵌⵍⵓⴶⵠⵏⴶ ⵢⵌⵠⵌⴽⵌⵀ

DRYDEN VOS & CRIMSON DAWN

CRIMINAL MASTERMINDS

The 'respectable' but temperamental face of Crimson Dawn, Dryden Vos is not someone to tangle with.

A ruthless criminal organization—even by other criminals' standards—the emerging Crimson Dawn is a lucrative syndicate of which Dryden Vos is a senior member and the public face.

A tall, imposing figure combined with the distinguishing striation markings on his face (which become more evident when his circulation and adrenaline levels increase) gives him the appearance of a terrifying adversary. His weapon of choice— a pair of customized Kyuzo petars which are specially designed to fit his human fingers and thumb claw —are particularly lethal.

Vos wears the Crimson Dawn signet ring as a sign of his allegiance to the syndicate. Awarded to only the most trusted members of the organization, it's clear that he has friends in high places, but exactly who they are remains a closely guarded secret.

Presenting himself as a cultured businessman with wide and varied tastes, Vos appears to be a benevolent host, rubbing shoulders with galactic leaders, celebrities, and professional party-goers, but behind closed doors he negotiates dark deals with criminal underlords and hatches terrible plans. Like an old-style gangster, Vos embraces the glamor of criminality, refusing to live life in the shadows. He enjoys the biggest and the best of everything, wears custom hand-made silk suits that even Lando Calrissian would be envious of, and travels the galaxy in no-expense-spared luxury.

Unfortunately for his numerous business associates, Vos is a true Jekyll and Hyde character, who can transform from a cultured gentleman to a cut-throat killer in an instant.

A symbol of the power of the syndicate, the *First Light* (an opulent Kalevalan star yacht) is a towering, dagger-shaped ship which bears the black and gold logo of its criminal owners. An imposing sight from the exterior, the inside is a riot of decadence where master chefs provide mouth-watering feasts while live music is performed by resident artiste, Aurodia Ventafoli.

Comprised of six large viewing decks, staterooms, Vos' study filled with antiquities, ample crew quarters and much-more, the *First Light* is an impressive sight as it travels through the galaxy. ●

PAUL BETTANY

Crime lord Dryden Vos marks a rare villainous role for acclaimed actor Paul Bettany.

How did you secure your role in *Solo*?
I have never asked anybody for a job ever, but the truth of how I got this job is that I texted Ron Howard saying, "Hey, Ron, have you ever spent long wintery evenings wondering why you're not in the *Star Wars* movies?" And my old mate Ron, with whom I've worked before, came through for me. About a week later, he said to come and play *Star Wars* with him.

What does Ron Howard bring to the *Star Wars* franchise?
Ron brings a lot of things. He is brilliant at understanding tone. He's also a master at knowing what he is making, and how far he can push a scene. As a director who is an actor, he's able to come in and solve any problems with a scene.

What makes Alden Ehrenreich so right for Han Solo?
The only thing I'd seen Alden in was *Hail Caesar!* (2016), the Coen brothers' movie, and I thought he walked away with the film. When I met him, I found him to be really personable and charming. He was helped a lot by the fact that the script feels like Han. It's got the tone right. But Alden understood who Han is.

> " While it's still a hero's journey, it is a heist caper with more humor in it than a lot of *Star Wars* movies. "

How did you enjoy working with Emilia Clarke?
She's so lovely. She went to the same drama school as me in London, so we had a very similar education in acting, and we work in very similar ways.

What does *Solo* add to *Star Wars* lore?
I love these offshoot movies that Lucasfilm are doing. It's a *Star Wars* movie, but *Solo* has a different tone. It's still a hero's journey, but it is a heist caper with more humor in it than a lot of *Star Wars* movies have been afforded time for in their stories.

How has working on *Solo* lived up to your expectations of playing a role in the *Star Wars* universe?
I can say I became an actor because of John Cassavetes' movies, but I'd really be lying! I saw *Star Wars* in 1978 and my life changed. I went to see it every day for a week. My parents thought I was crazy! Ever since, I've been a fan.

It's been brilliant to finally be in a *Star Wars* movie. I was able to bring my 14-year-old son to the set and take him aboard the *Millennium Falcon*. It was really something. We were both like, "Oh, that's the chess table." For the pair of us, it was a special time. ●

3 /

1 / Paul Bettany strikes
a pose as the Crimson
Dawn frontman. (See
previous spread)

2 / Dryden Vos lets
his displeasure show.
(See opposite page)

3 / The increasing striation
on Vos' face is a tell-tale
sign that there's trouble
ahead.

4 / Vos observes the
revellers onboard the
First Light.

4 /

5

6 /

7 /

8 /

5 / Hylobon goons bearing the emblem of Crimson Dawn are employed by Vos to provide security on the ship. (See opposite page)

6 / Dryden Vos appreciates rare antiquities—like the rare Mandalorian suit of armor seen in the background.

7/ Beckett, Han and Chewie receive a 'friendly' word of warning.... Will they take notice?

8 / Dryden Vos issues orders to his trusted lieutenant, Qi'ra.

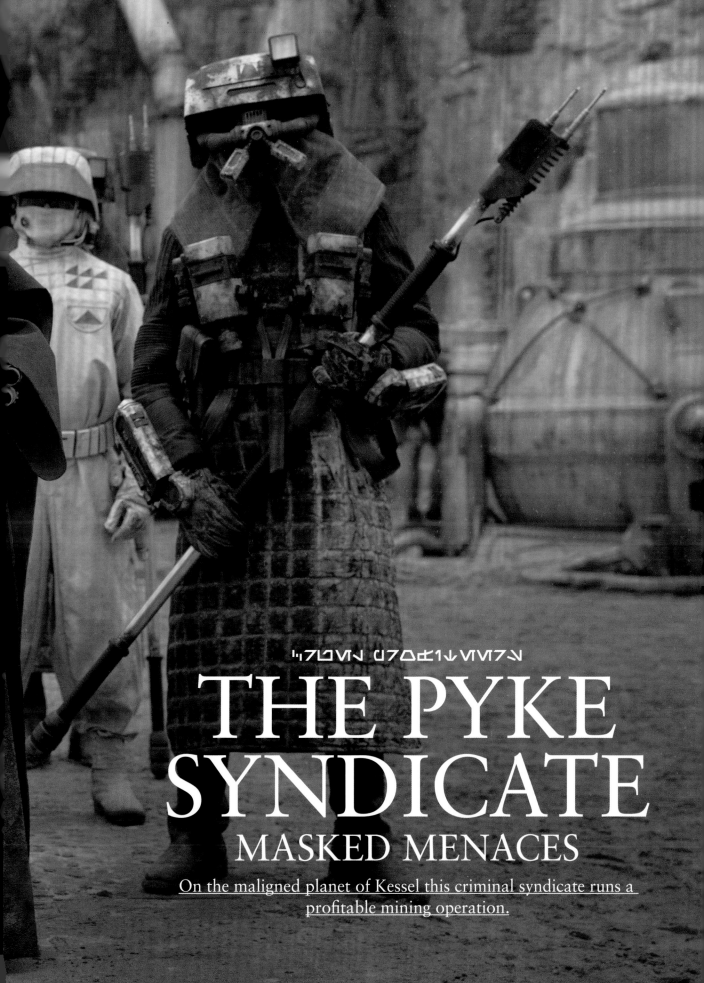

ᴉ⅃ᘓᐯᴎ ᘌᘓᗉᗉᗉᘿᖷᴎᐯ ᐯᐯᴎᘌᗉᐯ

THE PYKE
SYNDICATE
MASKED MENACES

On the maligned planet of Kessel this criminal syndicate runs a profitable mining operation.

2 /

1 / Director of Pyke mining operations on Kessel, Quay Tolsite and his sentries guard the entrance to the fabled Kessel spice mines. (See previous page)

2 / Clad in masks and clothes to protect them from the toxic by-products of the mining process, the villainous Pykes have an ominous appearance.

3 / Pyke sentries guard the precious haul recovered from the mines.

4 / Defending the coveted and valuable spice mines (which occasionally also throw up veins of rare coaxium—the valuable hyperdrive fuel), against burglars, would-be competitors, and smugglers is par for the course for the Pyke Syndicate. (See opposite page)

O riginally from nearby Oba Diah, the villainous Pyke Syndicate establishes an operational base on Kessel after striking a mutually profitable deal with the planet's King Yaruba. The agreement enables the Syndicate to mine half the planet for spice, a naturally occurring medicinal mineral highly valued by members of the criminal underworld, transforming it into a powerful narcotic. As sole exploiters of the valuable Kessel mines, it's a deal that makes the greedy Syndicate highly envied by other criminal gangs throughout the galaxy.

Always eager to see what is being recovered from the mines, the Empire allows the Syndicate to continue running their mining operation whilst keeping them under surveillance. In return for supplying prisoners to work as slaves, the Empire receives some of the valuable minerals and materials from the operation, which go toward strengthening the Imperial war machine.

The mines of Kessel are a desperate place, full of toxic pools, noxious gasses, intense heat and such terrible working conditions that many consider being sent there the worst punishment in the galaxy. Indiscriminate of race or age, the prisoners working the mines come in all guises—from con-artists and traitors to kidnapped schoolchildren. However, the most valuable among these are Wookiees and Gigorans, whose natural strength and powerful build render them extremely useful.

In order to keep costs low and profit margins high,

3 /

the Pykes also make use of an entire droid workforce to not only toil in the bleak mines, but as adminmechs to run the operations center. Tasked with monitoring prisoners and their progress at all times, the droids are fitted with strong restraining bolts to prevent them from leaving their posts or stepping out of line.

Being sole profiteers of the Kessel mining operation has made the Pykes wealthy and influential, but has also left them vulnerable to attack from competitors, smugglers and traders keen to get a cut of the spice trade. As a result, the Pykes employ armed thugs to act as sentinels to keep watch for any prisoners causing unrest, or for smugglers attempting to escape the system with something they shouldn't be carrying. Outfitted in lead-lined coats to protect against radiation and sealed helmets to filter out atmospheric toxins, they are an imposing sight.

However, smugglers and other criminal competitors are not the only hazard of life on Kessel. The toxins released into the planet's atmosphere during the mining process have a degenerative effect on everything— from living creatures to objects and even weapons, which deteriorate under the ever-present Kesselstone dust. Ironically, the Pykes' delicate physical makeup is vulnerable to the harsh conditions of the planet, and many are forced to keep their distance. Quay Tolsite, the director of operations, is the only high-ranking Pyke official stationed on the planet. Above all, his concern is to turn a profit, and he cares little for the misery and suffering of the prisoners working in the mines. ●

ᒐᕝᔑᕂᐧᐯ᠋ᒋᐃᓗᕋᐧ ᒥᕀᒋᕝᒥ ᙓᐃᐧᕀᕀ

ENFYS NEST & THE CLOUD-RIDERS

THE WILD LEADER

This enigmatic warrior leads the swoop-mounted Cloud-Rider pirate gang in their plundering missions.

A ferocious, mysterious warrior and a thorn in the side of Dryden Vos, Enfys Nest possesses a broad range of martial arts skills and styles which are impressively showcased in combat. However, apart from Nest's reputation as a fearsome adversary, little else is known about the outlaw owing to the all-concealing mask, ample armor and cloak which shrouds their body at all times—therefore making it extremely difficult to pinpoint the species, origins or even the gender of the pirate. While speculation about the being behind the mask is rife, whoever it is goes to great lengths to conceal their identity—even wearing a vocorder box to disguise their real voice.

A capable adversary, the lead Cloud-Rider isn't afraid to demonstrate their combat skills and prefers melee weapons, like the electroripper staff, over blasters. Using the staff, the masked marauder is able to deliver a range of powerful swipes and jabs showcasing their physical prowess while intimidating less-skilled opponents. Quick and surefooted, the agile Nest is also able to make impressive leaps (aided by repulsorlift boosters worn on the leg), to close distances or gain an advantage over an enemy. In all, the weapons and outfit combine to make a powerful and formidable warrior.

Nest seems to have a particular hostility toward Crimson Dawn operations and has long been a recurring problem for the criminal gang. While the outlaw's motives may be hidden, the mysterious character undoubtedly poses a real threat to the organized crime syndicates.

THE CLOUD-RIDERS

A marauding gang mounted on swoop bikes, the Cloud-Riders prey on cargo transports on some of the toughest planets in the galaxy. A group of outlaws, all of them generally conceal their true identities behind masks.

A nomadic group, the Cloud-Riders travel the Outer Rim Territories aboard their carrier ship, the *Aerie*. They can mainly be found haunting the skies of Vandor, but as pirates constantly on the search for vessels to plunder, they follow the route of valuable cargos.

The gang ride swoop bikes—a notoriously difficult vehicle to pilot, amounting to little more than an engine with seats—which are decorated with the gang's bold colors. To be a swoop pilot requires strength, timing and good instincts—something the Cloud-Riders all display.

While they are pirates, their prime objective is to capture their prey rather than destroy it, and their weapons —such as the portable ordnance launchers they carry—are intended to immobilize rather than injure adversaries. ●

1 / The mysterious and dangerous Enfys Nest. (See previous page)

2 / Enfys Nest and Tobias Beckett confer on the beach on Savareen.

3 / A swoop bike, ideal for when you need to get somewhere, fast.

2 /

3 /

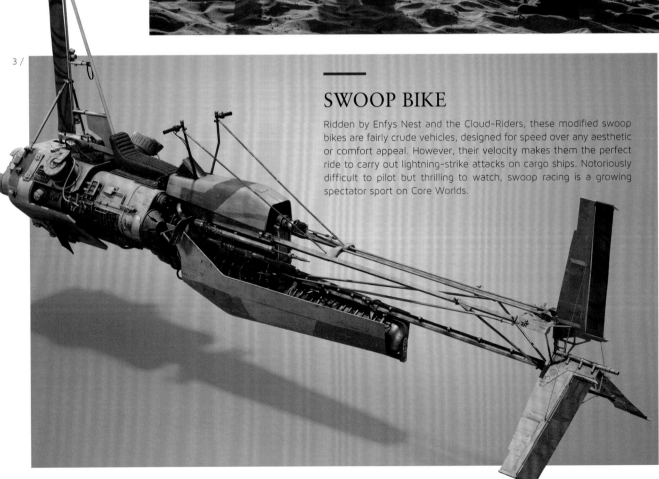

SWOOP BIKE

Ridden by Enfys Nest and the Cloud-Riders, these modified swoop bikes are fairly crude vehicles, designed for speed over any aesthetic or comfort appeal. However, their velocity makes them the perfect ride to carry out lightning-strike attacks on cargo ships. Notoriously difficult to pilot but thrilling to watch, swoop racing is a growing spectator sport on Core Worlds.

4 / The Cloud-Riders, a band of criminals not to be crossed.

STORMTROOPERS
SOLDIERS OF THE EMPIRE

As the Imperial machine expands throughout the galaxy, its army of stormtroopers diversifies to meet the challenges of the new worlds it hopes to conquer.

RANGETROOPER

These specialized stormtroopers, some of the toughest in the Imperial ranks, are deployed to rugged settlements—such as the snow-covered planet of Vandor—to protect Imperial interests. They wear heavy-duty magnetomic gription boots (used for maintaining grip on high-velocity conveyex), a syth fur-lined kama and suit to protect against the cold, and a helmet which features larger, tougher components than the standard helmets. They also carry BlasTech E-10R blaster rifles with enhanced infrared optics and stabilizer, which are more durable than the standard E-11.

IMPERIAL SWAMP TROOPER (AKA MUDTROOPER)

The Imperial troops battling in the difficult conditions on Mimban wear uniforms designed for the particular challenges that the planet's swampy atmosphere presents. In addition to sealed undersuits, damp-proof boots, partial armor and flared, high-impact plastoid helmets with built-in respirators, they're also issued with respirator masks and goggles.

PATROL TROOPER

These specialist urban stormtroopers police the streets of large, sprawling cities—like those found on Corellia. Their partial armor allows more movement than the full-body suits of standard stormtroopers, and the enlarged helmet dome features a built-in comlink to their HQ, which provides them with real-time traffic data, enabling them to swiftly navigate the city. They're equipped with a lightweight EC-17 hold-out blaster pistol and ride Aratech C-PH patrol speeder bikes.

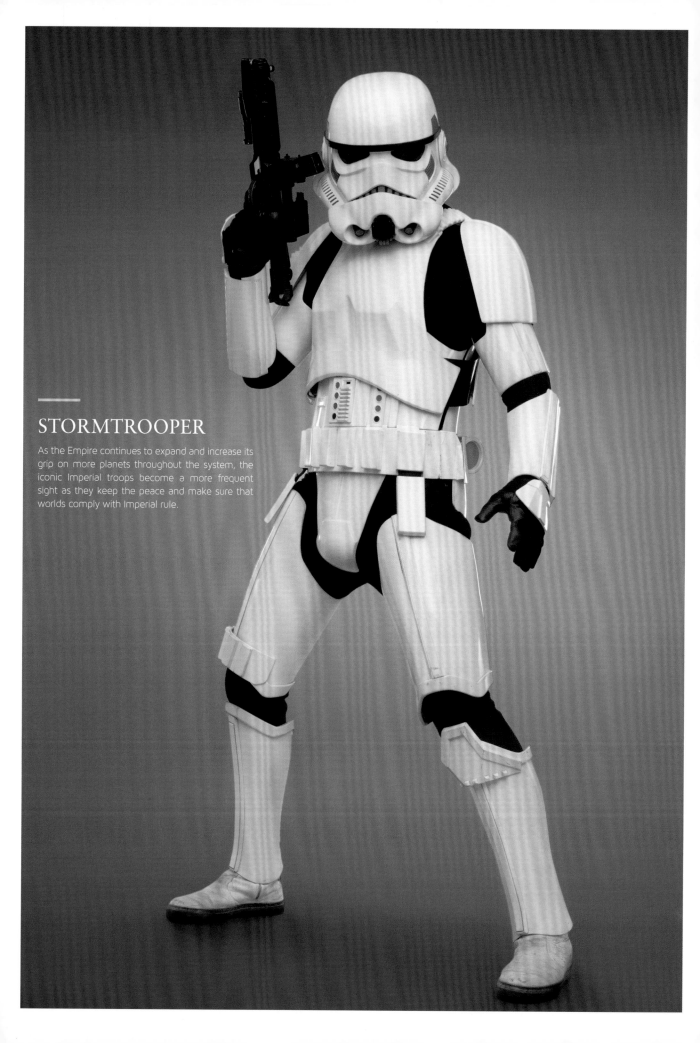

STORMTROOPER

As the Empire continues to expand and increase its grip on more planets throughout the system, the iconic Imperial troops become a more frequent sight as they keep the peace and make sure that worlds comply with Imperial rule.

WET-WEATHER GEAR
STORMTROOPER

For "pacification" duty on the conflict-ridden planet Mimban, standard stormtroopers have received minor modifications to their armor to help them cope with the adverse conditions. Waterproof capes known as "slicks" help ward off excess mud, while their helmets are fitted with enhanced targeting sensors to identify heat signatures through the persistent mists that often shroud the planet.

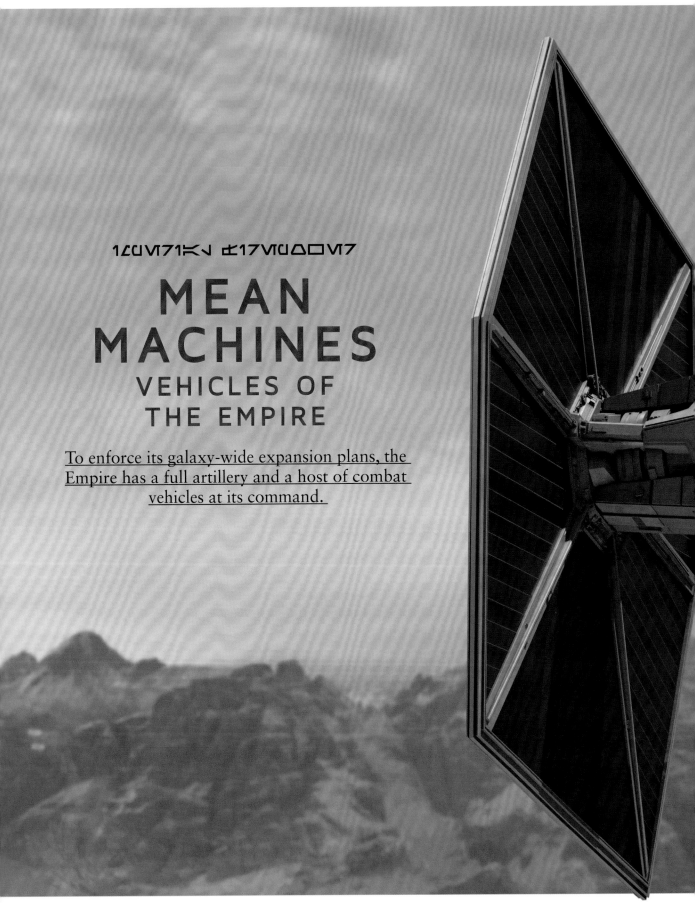

ᒪᔑᐅᐫᔨᑎᐠᒐ ᕼᕯᔨᐫᑕᐊᐅᐫᔨᒐ

MEAN MACHINES
VEHICLES OF
THE EMPIRE

To enforce its galaxy-wide expansion plans, the
Empire has a full artillery and a host of combat
vehicles at its command.

TIE/RB HEAVY STARFIGHTER

This new incarnation of the Empire's iconic TIE fighter has earned itself the nickname of the TIE "brute" thanks to its heavier armor and firepower. Fitted with pivoting self-powered SFS H-s9.3 twin laser cannons and triple-laminated, quadranium-reinforced titanium armor, they're also equipped with an MGK-300 integrated droid intelligence, similar to their more traditional astromech counterparts.

AT-DT

The All Terrain Defense Turret is a vehicle used to control Imperial ground installations, and comes fitted with heavy armor plating and artillery flashback shielding.

While not as intimidating as AT-ATs or AT-STs, it nevertheless represents another example of the Empire's might on the battlefield.

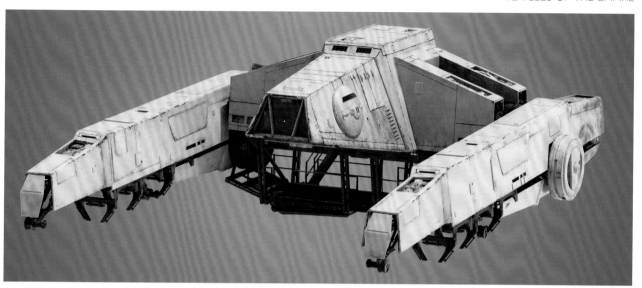

AT-HAULER

Navigated by both a pilot and co-pilot, AT-haulers are utilized by the Empire to transport walker vehicles on to the battlefield. Featuring two long propulsion and lifter arms powered by ion engines and repulsorlift generators, the AT-haulers are extremely strong and able to withstand very heavy loads. When grounded, the hauler's wings rotate skyward to save space, which is beneficial in hangar bays or planet side.

IMPERIAL PATROL SPEEDER

A common sight on the streets of large cities such as Coronet, the big and bulky Aratech C–PH is piloted by Imperial patrol troopers tasked with local law enforcement. Equipped with a forward fixed blaster cannon, it's designed for power over agility—although it is still able to reach impressive speeds of up to 399 kph.

CONVEYEX

These long, windowless, heavily armored vehicles travel on rails across inhospitable terrains and are used by the Empire to transport particularly valuable cargo which requires tight security (such as highly valuable coaxium). The cargo cars are fitted with blast doors and code-key locks. Made up of three sections—a front engine, a chain of cargo containers, and a rear-stabilizing caboose—the conveyex also features two medium repeating laser cannons and one double anti-aircraft laser turret. They are (supposedly) highly impenetrable.

ᚲ ᚢᚱᚲᚨᚢ ᚢᚱ ᚲᛜᚤᚡᛁᚨᛃᚢᚦᛗ

CREATING GALAXIES, FAR, FAR AWAY...

The filming of *Solo: A Star Wars Story* took place at Pinewood Studios in the U.K., and at two additional locations: the Dolomites in Italy and Fuerteventura in the Canary Islands. The task of designing these worlds fell to production designer and *Star Wars* veteran Neil Lamont. The team who helped him bring some unexplored worlds to life included Gary Tomkins (senior art director), Alastair Bullock (supervising art director), and Dominic Tuohy (special effects supervisor).

2 /

What did you think when you first saw the script for *Solo*?

Neil Lamont (production designer): It's such an aspirational story and a journey of such scope for the characters. It was a fantastic creative opportunity to discover and design, build and show audiences such diverse settings, and to realize environments that have been spoken about so often in previous films.

You were able to refer to material from Ralph McQuarrie and Joe Johnston, *Star Wars*' original concept artists. How did that help?

NL: We cast our research net far and wide, and kept returning to the themes of the Western genre again and again, and it weaves itself in and out of each of the sets as a theme and as an overall look.

How much of the original look did you limit yourselves to?

Alastair Bullock (supervising art director): We tried to keep the original aesthetic, or at least the spirit of the original aesthetic, while upgrading the build quality

and the finishes to modern standards to adhere to the scrutiny and expectation of today's audiences.

CORELLIA

Han's home planet is an industrial version of Venice, connected by bridges. What inspired that approach?

NL: We asked ourselves how they would create such big spacecraft in this world. It just came about that we felt so much could be done over water, by creating these different islands with different functions—administrative or industrial or residential, all interconnected by bridges and roads.

You built Corellia at Pinewood Studios and at Fawley Power Station in England. What made you build on location rather than build these places on a studio set?

NL: We could never have afforded, nor had the space, to build a set that had so much technical depth within it. Once we had found Fawley, and it gave us the concrete structures, the broken-down piping, the

beginning of the film, so it looks like it's been around the block, had a history before he's acquired it. But it has been engineered like a racing car. It drives like a real racing car, and it could do well over a hundred miles an hour.

There was also a speeder chasing Han created for the chase—how did that take shape?
GT: In terms of both design and color, the speeder needed to feel intimidating to Han during the chase, so we worked on the basis of a heavy truck, with a front grille with a great big bull bar, which would feel really menacing behind you.

What was the train of thought for the design and build process?
GT: It was very quirky. Moloch drives in a little cage in the middle of the vehicle; toward the front there's a cage with dogs. The creature effects department made two animatronic dogs, so when the car is speeding along, you can see the dogs snarling and growling in the cage to add to the sense of intimidation.

What made this chase sequence different?
Dominic Tuohy (special effects supervisor): The speeder chase really excited me about this project. We've seen a lot of chases within the *Star Wars* franchise but we have never seen a speeder chase like this. Part of the car chase was showing Han's driving skills as well as his flaws, so we had him hitting things that would explode to keep the audience guessing as to whether he's in control or not.

How did you create the Den of the White Worms set at Pinewood Studios?
Alastair Bullock (supervising art director): We created a stagnant underground chamber in an old industrial plant. The concrete nature of the set reflects the brutality of Lady Proxima, and the community of lost boys and girls, who must perform these dastardly deeds on her behalf, in return for her protection.

What was the thinking behind the spaceport set that was constructed at Pinewood Studios?
NL: The idea was to show a mixture of the crumbling old Corellian architecture and how aspirational Corellia was before it became an Empire-occupied territory. We bought into this concrete feel, given we were using the concrete structures at Fawley for our exteriors, and showed Corellia's faded elegance tonally with the murals running along the side of the set, illustrating early space flight, remnants of a bygone area, juxtaposed with the familiar Imperial elements.

The set needed to be enormous. It filled the 007 stage at Pinewood Studios. It amplifies Han's vulnerability; a very small boy lost and alone in this huge space, and on the run.

general dirty and rusty feel we wanted, the location very much became a foundation to how we imagined the rest of Corellia.

One of the biggest scenes on Corellia is Han's speeder chase. How did that design come about?
Gary Tomkins (senior art director): We based the design on the American muscle car from the late '60s/early '70s, combined with speeder technology, and taking design cues from Luke's speeder in *A New Hope* and other craft seen in the *Star Wars* universe.

What choices were made to find Han's speeder?
GT: Many concepts, designs and models by teams working in both the U.K. and the U.S. were produced, and after a long process the team arrived at a design that made everyone happy. The filmmakers decided the speeder should be blue with white racing stripes, and a little beaten up.

What was the first thing the team agreed on?
GT: From an early stage, everyone wanted a quirky, rather than slick-looking, vehicle. Han steals it at the

1 / Han Solo on Mimban, a location first mentioned as far back as 1979 in the *Star Wars* Legends novel, *Splinter of the Mind's Eye.* (See previous spread)

2 / Stormtroopers on patrol on Corellia.

3 / An encampment on the muddy world of Mimban.

4 / Beckett, Han and Chewie traverse the icy planet, Vandor.

3 /

VANDOR

A reduced unit traveled to the Dolomites in Italy for a six-day shoot, and cast and crew took over the small village of Misurina—what were the conditions like?

Thandie Newton (Val): I'm always humbled by the kinds of experiences we have doing this job. In the Dolomites, in that vista, being tiny specks among those incredible mountains was quite wonderful. It was like being at camp with the *Star Wars* team. I absolutely loved it. It's such a gift to the audience to see this extraordinary landscape, to be reminded that there are places in the world that are so magnificent and unspoiled.

The Fort Ypso saloon has a very similar vibe to the Mos Eisley cantina. But it's also a *Star Wars* first, isn't it?

4 /

NL: I think the saloon is the first example of wooden architecture in *Star Wars* [not including Wookiees' and Ewoks' treehouses]. It had good circulation, it had good depth, and from that we then worked in the other areas, namely the sabacc room and the droid-fight area.

How did you approach dressing the set?

Lee Sandales (set decorator): The saloon is in an outlaw town, in a very harsh alpine environment, and we dressed it with those cues in mind. We started with the most basic theme, that it should be a wooden structure, with wood furniture. Vandor is cold, so they would need stoves, and, based on the side of the mountain, they would have their own brewery, because they couldn't be bringing goods in too often.

It's a *Star Wars* tradition to use found objects. Did that continue for *Solo*?

LS: We found these really amazing 1930s Swiss toboggans in an antiques market in the South of France. They were just perfect. They look like *Star Wars* sledges. We didn't need to do anything to them. In Mos Eisley the optics behind the bar are the flame cans from a jet engine. I found some broken ones in the breakage yard and used them here. It's a small but lovely added connection between the two films.

MIMBAN

How did you create the Mimban mud planet?

NL: Mimban is a planet being assailed by the Empire as they oppress an indigenous race. It's a battlefield with a lot of fog and a lot of smoke, so we could get away with a big painted backing, again using the 007 Stage, with a horizon of a cloudy sky. We used that huge space to put in craters, ruins, and created camps with tents. We had a lot of fun with this set.

How did you make it feel war-torn and real?

DT: We introduced rockets and live explosions. Everything was practical. Nothing was for show. It really feels like we're in the middle of it.

You used gray shale, sourced from a Welsh quarry, to dress the Mimban sets. What was that like?

AB: We had a mountain of it on the backlot, which we would just keeping digging into to dress the Mimban sets. The 007 Stage at one time was completely covered in gray slate.

KESSEL

There's a lot of yellow going on in Kessel...

AB: The idea is that the spice is everywhere. It's in the ducting. It's very corrosive, so this was a great set to do in terms of the crusty and rich finishes that we could play with. Goodness knows how many dustbins we filled with yellow sawdust, but it looked really good.

How did you design a practical light source for the interior mines set?

LS: I came across an early concept for Cloud City [by Ralph McQuarrie]. It had a tiny aerial at the top. I turned it upside down, and it looked like a mining lamp. It was just a tiny little sketch, but it prompted the design for all the lights in the Kessel Mines.

5 /

SAVAREEN

What was required from the location used to depict Savareen in the film?
NL: We knew we needed to go to an extraordinary environment to capture it. It's our 'High Noon.' It's the final confrontation.

Location filming for this was in Fuerteventura, the second largest of Spain's Canary Islands, over 12 weeks. What did this location bring to the film?
AB: It was stunning to see the set materialize out of this landscape. It's a beautiful landscape, with this dune running directly down on a big slope to this dramatic and windswept rocky coastline. It's one of those sets that, when you're in the middle of it, it's a complete environment, a 360-degree set. You are really in that refinery.

What was the idea behind it?
LS: The idea is that a small nomadic tribe have moved in, and are living among the ruins of this ghost town. We came up with themes of what they would do if they actually lived there, and expanded these themes into a culture.

We imagined they were fishermen and that they lived on fish. The shells had given them the gift of forms of dye, which they combined with flax from a local farm to weave and make canopies, which we used all around the set. ●

6 /

5 / Droids in control on Kessel.

6 / Beckett and Han in conference on Savareen.

SCOUNDREL STYLE

What's in a look? Quite a lot, particularly when the costume team—headed by David Crossman and Glyn Dillon—needed to create over 1,000 outfits.

What attracted you to working on *Solo*?
David Crossman (costume designer): Han Solo is my favorite character from the original trilogy films. He's just the epitome of cool. He has such an iconic look to explore.

Were you excited by the challenges of the script?
Glyn Dillon (costume designer): The characters that Han meets throughout his journey are so layered and so rich that they presented fantastic opportunities for us as designers.

What makes a *Star Wars* costume?
DC: It's something real that audiences can relate to from their own life and from history, mixed with fantasy elements, which give it the *Star Wars* feel.

You took inspiration from original designs, as well as other 1970s references, often Western ones, including Robert Altman's *McCabe & Mrs Miller* (1971). What was the thought process?
DC: Han Solo's look is such a classic, iconic one, so we didn't want to veer too far away from the original costume, but we wanted to see how he got there. We liked the idea that the look becomes Han Solo during the course of the film as he acquires pieces from Beckett, and from other characters. The more people he meets, the more he gathers and establishes his own identity.

What was the inspiration for Han's first look, when he is a street urchin on Corellia?
GD: We were looking at bands like The Clash for inspiration, and we arrived at a 1980s punk look mixed with a 1950s element.

It works as a negative of his classic costume. The vest is white, the shirt is dark and the Corellian trouser strip is faintly visible. He's identifiable as Han Solo. The punkish, 1950s-inspired version of the iconic costume suggests youth and rebellion.

Tell us about the mudtrooper outfit?
DC: Han wears the standard Imperial uniform, for which we've taken some elements from *The Empire Strikes Back* helmets and created a quasi-stormtrooper goggle and capes reminiscent of Russian ones from the World Wars. The boots are Han's, which he carries on through his journey.

By the time he is reunited with Qi'ra on Dryden's Yacht, he's starting to look almost like the Han Solo everyone knows.

Was Han's suede jacket a deliberate nod to his outfit in *A New Hope*?
DC: There was a lovely '60s jacket we saw somewhere in London, with black paneling, on which we based the suede jacket. The original Han Solo look in *A New Hope* was very cropped, so we aimed for that look, keeping the sleeves shorter, the jacket length cropped, so it's clear for the guns.

For Lando, the designers turned to musical influences like Jimi Hendrix, Prince, and Marvin Gaye—why was that?
GD: He's such a colorful character. We wanted to have fun with his costumes and bring in very strong colors and some vibrancy.

Usually it can take a while for various costumes to be designed, but wasn't Lando's look decided upon quite quickly?

▶

2 /

3 /

> "
> # There has to be something in the way [Qi'ra] dresses that gives her that ambiguous edge.
> "
> ## - Glyn Dillon

GD: In one of the first drawings we did of Lando, we drew him with a yellow shirt, and that was it. That was Lando.

What was the thinking behind Lando's extensive cape collection?
DC: In the closet, we tried to incorporate every texture possible, mixings and patterns, velvets and leathers, just to get a great variety, as audiences won't see Lando in much else than his yellow shirt.

Why did you create such a sharp contrast between Qi'ra's Corellian look and her glamorous, First Light outfit?
GD: Qi'ra's Corellian outfit is quite '80s punk, with an oversized boyfriend jacket, leather skirt, and pointy boots. We opted for more of a femme fatale look when Han is reunited with her later in the movie. We wanted to create a look that would blow Han away when he sees her. She has to be recognizable, but there has to be something in the way she dresses that gives her that ambiguous edge: is she dangerous, can he trust her?

How did you achieve that look?
DC: She's second-in-command of this criminal gang. Her look needed to be sophisticated, so we went with a beautiful Lauren Bacall-inspired black silk dress. We gave it powerful shoulders, and shiny black jewelry, that incorporates the Crimson Dawn logo.

What was your inspiration for Beckett's costume design?
GD: We wanted to give Beckett that mentor feel for Han. He wears a pale, long duster coat over a dark flight suit.

He's one of the few characters that doesn't really change his clothes.
DC: Beckett wears the costume almost throughout. The script might dictate that, but sometimes it's helpful for certain characters too. People identify with them better.

Why did you decide to have Beckett wearing Lando's armor from *Return of the Jedi* in one sequence?
GD: It's the helmet that was based on a baseball glove, and it was great fun recreating that costume

1 / Han's suede jacket allows easy access to his trusty blaster. (See previous spread)

2 / Qi'ra's elegant femme fatale outfit, intended to "blow Han away."

3 / Modeling the '80s punk look on Corellia.

4 / Dressed for trouble, blaster at her side. (See opposite page)

6 /

5 / Lando Calrissian's outfit drew inspiration from Prince, Marvin Gaye, and Jimi Hendrix. (See opposite page)

6 / Thandie Newton strikes a pose as Val wearing her "punky gear."

> "
> Val's strong and she's really cool, so we went with a backward apron skirt that is really *Star Wars* and quite punky.
> "
> - Glyn Dillon

▶ for Beckett. Hopefully it looks to fans like Beckett left it on the *Millennium Falcon*, and years later when Lando came back to the *Falcon* to rescue Han, he would have dug it out and remembered it was the one Beckett used years before. It's one of those connecting elements that *Star Wars* fans love.

What did you think of the Val character?
GD: Val was a fun one to do. Val's strong and she's cool, so we went with leather and the backward apron skirt that is really *Star Wars*, and also quite punky.

How did you go about establishing a look for Dryden Vos?
GD: There had to be a connection between Dryden and Qi'ra that presents itself as a threat to Han. It's not just a physical threat but a romantic one also. This was something we felt was important to express in Dryden's costume. He needed to look charming and suave, but dangerous too.

You also created non-conventional clothing too, in the form of L3-37, who was a collaboration between costume and visual effects. What are the key elements of her costume?
GD: The head is like the top of a dome of an astromech, but has been cut down. The shoulders are like the tops of the sides of the legs on an astromech droid, like an R2 unit. There are little vents and certain details that we're sure the fans have noticed.

How does it work in terms of the final digital effects used on Phoebe Waller-Bridge, who plays L3-37?
GD: Visual effects only took out her face, belly and arms, so she's able to interact and it looks real. The end result gives a different-looking, fully interactive character rather than a purely computer-generated one. ●

7 / L3-37: a droid built
by the costume and visual
effects departments.

8 / Han's Corellian outfit
hints at what later becomes
his signature vest.

1 /

ᒍᗐᐯᓰ ᐯᓀᗐᓀᐯᓰᐟᒍᐯ

INDUSTRIAL LIGHT & MAGIC

There were more than 2,000 visual effects on *Solo*. The man in charge of pulling them together was visual effects supervisor and co-producer Rob Bredow from Industrial Light & Magic. Alongside a global team of 1,200 artists and technicians, he created vehicles, character performances, otherworldly environments, and unique spacecraft.

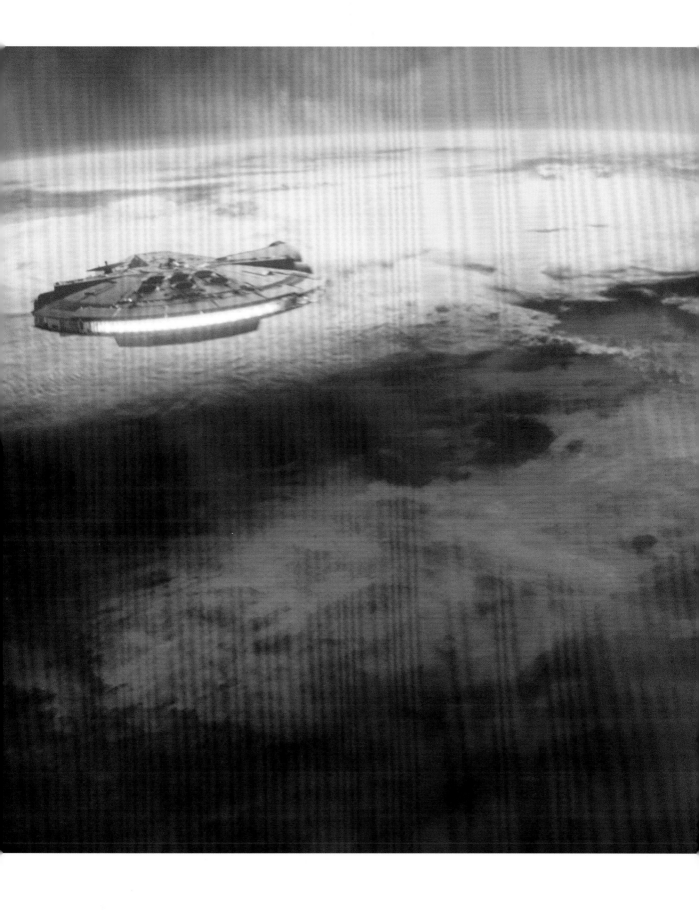

Did the effects demands on Solo push you to new limits?
Rob Bredow: (visual effects supervisor and co-producer) I think we pulled out every trick in the book on this film, and developed a few new ones of our own. We took some of the oldest visual effects techniques, such as front- and rear-screen projection, and updated them with the latest technology. This allowed us to film 360-degree environments on the stunning Dryden's Yacht set.

What kind of new techniques did you adopt on this film?
We used the latest laser projection technology to surround the *Falcon* cockpit with screens. When we immersed the cast into hyperspace, they were actually experiencing it like you would on a simulator ride. Only this was at a feature-film quality that worked in-camera.

You combined rod puppets and creature costumes with state-of-the-art digital effects to introduce new characters such as L3-37 and Rio Durant. How important was it to use practical characters?
We made every effort to capture as much in-camera as possible, not only for the creatures and environments but also the incredible vehicles in the film. Those are real 550-horsepower speeders, and we removed the wheels and enhanced the world around them using visual effects. Even Phoebe Waller-Bridge, who played L3-37, was wearing a practical costume on-set for the parts we didn't create digitally. We had it all there right in front of us when we shot, lit by Bradford's beautiful lighting and ready for Ron's direction. Our visual effects team could work from that base reality, always having the photography to ground the shots.

How do you feel about what you and the team have achieved on *Solo*?
It was such a privilege to take fans into the *Star Wars* universe. To do that we endeavored to utilize the best combination of modern technology and a 1970s filmmaking aesthetic. It's one of the things that makes *Solo* so unique. ●

2 /

3 /

1 / The *Millennium Falcon* soars over Kessel. (See previous spread)

2 / The conveyex hurtles across the surface of Vandor.

3 / Dryden Vos, a practical character with digitally created striations.

4 / The gambling den on Vandor.

4 /

SHOOTING SOLO

The lighting of a movie is vitally important in transporting the audience to another world—sometimes even another galaxy. Fortunately *Solo* had one of the best people on hand in the shape of director of photography Bradford Young.

1

What were your first thoughts when you read the script for *Solo*?

Bradford Young (director of photography): It was a script that played off the classics and had all the beautiful tropes and clichés of the original films.

One of the things that struck me was that the film had to feel natural; it had to feel earthbound, about characters putting their feet on natural surfaces. Everything had to be coming from the right place, whether it was where the camera was placed or where the light was coming from.

How do you achieve that on film?
If you want to feel, taste or smell the snow, or if you want to feel and taste the sand, nothing is better than allowing that sand or that snow to be lit by the sun or the moon.

Was it important for you to be able to highlight that realism?
Audiences are now really hyper-aware when things don't feel real. This film had to feel real. It's far more difficult to work that way, but it's something that I've trained myself to do. It's about finding the moment, finding the source, and then constructing the moment around that.

How did the sets themselves help you create realism?
Neil Lamont designed sets that allowed us to light from the set, so every practical light that you see in this film is actually lighting the subject. When the character steps away from the lighting source, they'll walk into the shadow. It might be a little intense for the audience for a moment, but the character will eventually step back into the light.

1 / Bradford Young lights
the *Solo* set. (See previous
spread)

2 / Beckett shoots his way
out of trouble on Mimban.

3 / The crew face the
challenge of the Kessel Run.

LIGHTING THE UNIVERSE:
WORKING WITH BRADFORD YOUNG

What do you think Bradford brings to Solo?
Alden Ehrenreich (Han Solo): I think Bradford's work is one of the key things that distinguishes *Solo* from the other *Star Wars* films. It's a much tougher, seedier world and story, and Bradford has lit it in a very organic and natural way, which gives the world an edge and a sense of danger. It doesn't feel glossy or removed.

What did you think of the lighting on Solo?
Simon Emanuel (producer): The director of photography can make the look of the film a real character in the story. Bradford's work is incredible. He truly is an artist who lights by instinct, and lights by how he feels looking at the particular scene or particular shot.

How did you find working with Bradford Young?
Thandie Newton (Val): I was very excited that Bradford was lighting the film. I'm a huge fan of the atmosphere he creates with light.

He brought a very interesting feel to the film. He's very consistent with how he wants to make the film look, and he has a very clear and recognizable style while at the same time keeping it in the world of *Star Wars* that audiences have come to expect. ●

5 /

6 /

4 / Qi'ra aboard the
First Light.

5 / Han attempts to
negotiate his way out
of trouble.

6 / Alden Ehrenreich lit
by Young's naturalistic
lighting style on the
Falcon set.

1 /

ᏝᏝᎧᏙᎥ⁴ ⅃ᏝᎧ⁊ ᏦᏗᎧ⅃ᏋᏙᎸ ᎠᏦᎫᏦᎧᏙ

SONIC SOLO

Composer John Powell has created a distinctive score
of original *Star Wars* music for *Solo*, which also includes
a new piece of work from the legendary composer
John Williams.

What inspiration did you take from John Williams' work?
John Powell (composer): There is a certain musical language that John Williams used in the *Star Wars* films, and I've tried to live up to the quality of what he had done before by keeping form and structure within the score and following the storytelling as honestly and elegantly as possible.

What inspired you most from the original score?
There is a lot of thematic material from the original movies that I used that was not specific to Han. It was specific to the *Millennium Falcon*, TIE fighters, and the Empire. Those types of things are very useful, as they're all part of the language we know. There are lots of other characters and ideas within the film that I wrote tunes and melodies for, so it's a mixture of new tunes, a new piece by John Williams and some of the old material.

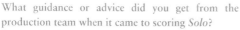

What guidance or advice did you get from the production team when it came to scoring *Solo*?

My love for the scores that John had originally written meant that I was thoroughly familiar with them. The filmmakers let me understand that I essentially needed to score a heist film. Yes, it is a *Star Wars* film, but it's also a heist film and character piece.

Did scoring this film allow you to paint a different picture of the *Star Wars* universe?

In this particular film we were dealing with an underworld with pirates and gangsters. There's no quasi-religious nature to the film at all. It's closer to *The Italian Job* meets *The Godfather*. I tried to take everything I loved about the series to help tell this story and explain everything we thought we knew about the characters.

There's no Force present in *Solo*. Did that change how you approached scoring the movie?

The hole that is left in a *Star Wars* movie by not having the Force must be filled with the idea of love

2 /

being the Force. It's about the good and the bad side of love, and about friendship, family, hope, and wanting to be part of something.

The *Solo* score was recorded at Abbey Road Studios in London, and used the same size orchestra that John Williams used. Was that important to you?

I felt we needed to stay in that world to make sure that everything was matching. So it's a normal size orchestra with about 98 players in total. The only unusual thing I added to the mix was a Bulgarian women's choir, which has a very unusual chorale sound. I think it's very effective in the movie. It represents the strangely exotic nature of the marauder gang. It's a beautiful sound that I used in a very aggressive way. ●

1 / A musical interlude aboard the *First Light*.

2 / Marauder Enfys Nest— Bulgarian women's choir not pictured.

WIN, LOSE OR DRAW

As part of *Solo: A Star Wars Story*'s advertising campaign, leading agency
BOND created a stunning series of images of our heroes playing sabacc.

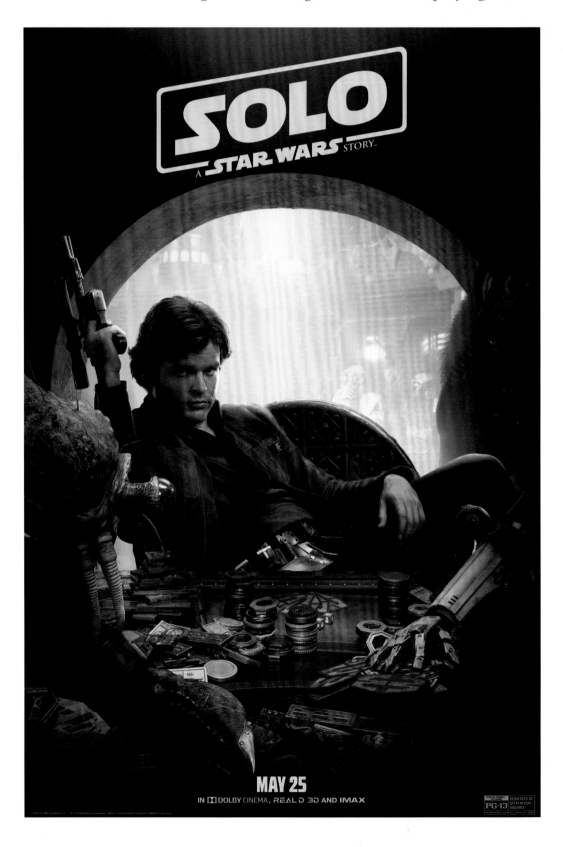

MAY 25

IN DOLBY CINEMA, REAL D 3D AND IMAX

PG-13

SEQUENCES OF
SCI-FI ACTION/
VIOLENCE

OTHER GREAT TIE-IN EDITIONS FROM TITAN
ON SALE NOW!

Rogue One: A Star Wars Story
The Official Collector's Edition
ISBN 9781785861574

Rogue One: A Star Wars Story
The Official Mission Debrief
ISBN 9781785861581

Star Wars: The Last Jedi
The Official Collector's Edition
ISBN 9781785862113

Star Wars: The Last Jedi
The Official Movie Companion
ISBN 9781785863004

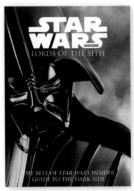

Rogue One: A Star Wars Story
The Official Collector's Edition
ISBN 9781785861574

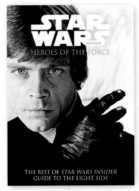

Star Wars:
Heroes of the Force
ISBN 9781785851926

Star Wars:
Icons Of The Galaxy
ISBN 9781785851933

The Best of Star Wars
Insider Volume 1
ISBN 9781785851162

The Best of Star Wars
Insider Volume 2
ISBN 9781785851179

The Best of Star Wars
Insider Volume 3
ISBN 9781785851896

The Best of Star Wars
Insider Volume 4
ISBN 9781785851902

Thor: Ragnarok
The Official Movie Special
ISBN 9781785851179

Black Panther
The Official Movie Special
ISBN 9781785866531

Avengers: Infinity War
The Official Movie Special
ISBN 9781785868054

Ant-Man and the Wasp
The Official Movie Special
ISBN 9781785868092

TITANCOMICS
For more information visit www.titan-comics.com